WORDS C

I support having the product reprinted and remastered, mainly because it is a document of Deaf lives and stories. The richness of the tales and live stories in this book are fabulous.

Ben Bahan, Ph.D.
Professor, Department of ASL and Deaf Studies, Gallaudet University, and Co-author, A Journey into the DEAF-WORLD

Scholars and students alike will benefit from this effort to preserve and promote these great stories. The wisdom of a people is in its literature and this wisdom, humor and craft should be preserved for generations to come.

Dirksen Bauman, Ph.D.
Professor, Department of ASL and Deaf Studies, Gallaudet University, and Author/Co-author, Deaf Gain: Raising the Stakes for Human Diversity, Open Your Eyes: Deaf Studies Talking, *and* Signing the Body Poetic: Essays in American Sign Language Literature

A Handful of Stories provides us with a meaningful glimpse into the lives of Deaf people—their experiences, expertise and above all, their humanity. Funny, insightful, heart-breaking and heart-warming. A mesmerizing must-read/view!

Linda Bove
Actress and Author, Sign Language Fun with Linda Bove

Back in the old days, many well-known and cherished storytellers developed important work and it's imperative that this book, *A Handful of Stories*, is not lost or taken away from generations yet to come. This is one book that will be on my bookshelf.

Deanne Bray-Kotsur, Actress and ASL Teacher

How exciting it is that *A Handful of Stories* is released again. A timeless classic, indeed! Roz does it again, another magical production, sharing the beauty of ASL, Deaf culture and the Deaf community.

Thomas K. Holcomb, Ph.D.
Professor, Deaf Studies Division, Ohlone College,
and Author, Introduction to American Deaf Culture
and Deaf Eyes on Interpreting

A Handful of Stories is unlike any other book! This production is narrated by diverse, renowned Deaf storytellers and filled with humor and heartfelt anecdotes that will leave you fulfilled, yet wanting more. I highly recommend obtaining a copy for your bookshelf, as it is indeed a classic.

Carolyn McCaskill, Ph.D.
Professor, Department of ASL and Deaf Studies,
Gallaudet University, and Co-author, The Hidden Treasure
of Black ASL, Its History and Structure

This history is an important part of understanding what Deaf Americans have experienced over the years. For many decades, hearing Americans have been unaware of Deaf people's journeys through life. This book is relevant to show what we have been through here in America. Read this book and learn from our best Deaf storytellers.

Janice Smith Warshaw, Ed.D.
Director of Deaf Studies Programs and Assistant Professor,
California State University, Fresno, and
American Sign Language Teachers Association President

A Handful of Stories

Seventy-four

Stories

by

Deaf Storytellers

Edited by Roz Rosen

Second Edition

Second Edition, 2018

*Originally published by the Division of Public Services
and Gallaudet University Press.*

Published by Savory Words Publishing
www.savorywords.com

ISBN 978-0-9863552-8-8
Printed in the United States of America

Dedicated to Deaf Narrators,
Past, Present, and Future

TABLE OF CONTENTS

INTRODUCTION

A few years ago, as I was selecting books to take with me when my husband Herb and I moved to California, I came across two books I had forgotten about: *A Handful of Stories* and *Another Handful of Stories*. Those books were relics from my past as the director of the Gallaudet College Special Schools of the Future (SSoF), a collaborative project among Gallaudet College and six schools for the deaf across the United States and Canada from 1979 unitl 1983. The purpose of this innovative project was to to collectively identify needs, issues, ideas and solutions, form functional networks to gather and share innovations among schools for the deaf. It sought to expand the capacity and visibility of those schools as statewide model programs and resource centers for continuing professional and community education to create better outcomes for Deaf students and people. Worthy activities, ideas, and solutions existed all over the United States.

I know I stray. But I wanted to you to know the background of this amazing and transformative project, launched just after P.L. 92-142 (the Education for All Handicapped Children Act) went into effect. This law is now known as the Individuals with Disabilities Education Act (IDEA). With the visionary leadership of Gallaudet College (now University) President Edward Merrill, Jr., and Vice President of Public Services Dr. Thomas Mayes, funding for the five-year SSoF project was made possible with the support of the W. K. Kellogg Foundation. I was chosen to direct the national SSoF project in 1979 and although I became the Dean of the College for Continuing Education in the division of public services in 1980, I continued to direct SSoF.

Two of the many pressing needs in the field were viable resources for language development as well as increasing self-esteem among Deaf students. As one way to get kids hooked on books and appreciative of their Deaf heritage, I decided to create *A Handful of Stories*, a book and videos of Deaf storytellers presenting glimpses into their lives and their thinking, experiences, and dreams. Students could read the stories in English and view the stories in American Sign

Language (ASL). The book and videos were so popular that we created the sequel, *Another Handful of Stories*. I served as the overall coordinator and editor, working with Bernard Bragg and Barbara Kannapell, who coordinated the storytellers, and with Ivy Pittle Wallace, who finalized the books. Some say this may have been the first known bilingual production ever.

As I blew the dust off the dog-eared 37-year-old books and gingerly turned the fragile pages, I was transported back in time, into the lives, thoughts and reflections of the Deaf community of yesteryear and of the individual Deaf storytellers, quite a number of whom have since passed on. The storytellers came from all walks of life; some were nationally recognized leaders and educators, and some were ordinary everyday people. All shared a zest for life.

In 1980, many things we now take for granted did not yet exist: captioned television, emails, smartphones with text and videos, video relay services, or even fax machines. Teachers proficient in American Sign Language (ASL) and English pedagogy were scarce, let alone professional interpreters. Bilingual education was yet to become an ideal; ASL had been identified as a bona fide language only in the 1960s by Dr. William Stokoe. Around 1980, "Total Communication" was coined by Dr. Roy Holcomb as a means to open the classroom door by a few inches to allow sign language, albeit in English order, to come in. In 1980, the National Association of the Deaf published a groundbreaking book by Jack Gannon, Deaf Heritage, to recognize and celebrate the many accomplishments of Deaf people. Even without adequate access and sometimes with improvised self-esteem regarding being Deaf or being sign language users, Deaf people gamely carried on with their daily lives in schools, communities and marketplaces.

Over the years, I found the stories in this book engrossing, relevant, thought-provoking and timeless. I checked with Gallaudet University Press to get a fresh copy of the book but was saddened to find out that the books were out of print with no intention of reprinting them.

Because there continues to this day a great void in bilingual materials and because of the continuing relevancy of these narrations, I asked for and was granted the right and privilege of repackaging the two volumes into one edition and publishing them along with the videos for modern-day audiences. The stories are presented exactly as they were in the original volumes.

It is interesting to note that the project coordinators, Bernard Bragg, Barbara Kannapell, and I were each born into Deaf families and are Gallaudet University alumni. They are treasures of the Deaf community, and I am grateful for their involvement in this project. Special gratitude also goes to Michael Olson of the Gallauet University Archives for his assistance with the photographs.

Great appreciation goes to Gallaudet University Press for releasing these materials to me, and to Savory Words Publishing and Trudy Suggs for her encouragement and partnership in publishing and distributing the new edition, thus putting this treasure back into your hands and into circulation for today's readers and viewers, teachers and students, families, historians, researchers, and many others.

Read on, be swept away into the far corners of history, and be captivated by the continuing relevance of these storytellers' narratives, experiences, and creativity. Enjoy!

Roz Rosen
Project Director, 1979-1983
Special Schools of the Future and AHandful of Stories
Dean, 1980-1993
Gallaudet University College for Continuing Education

FROM THE PUBLISHER

I grew up during the 1970s and 1980s (P.L. 94-142, now the Individuals with Disabilites Education Act, was enacted on my first birthday), and often scoured publications like *Silent News* and *World Around You* to read about Deaf people who paved the way for future generations. My stepfather was active in the Chicago Deaf community, and I often tagged along when he attended Frat or Illinois Association of the Deaf activities, watching renowned Deaf leaders discuss issues such as captioning, employment, telephone access, and so much more. The impressions that these Deaf individuals, along with the storytellers in this book, left upon me as a child and young adult have been everlasting.

The Deaf President Now protest took place in 1988, when I was 13. The following year, I attended Deaf Way. Both events changed my life; I realized that I was part of an amazing cultural and linguistic community. Soon after, the Americans with Disabilities Act was passed. As a wide-eyed teenager smack-dab in the middle of so many events in such a short time, I saw Deaf people's lives forever changed. Yet the stories in this book take place *before* all of these crucial milestones. As I read and watched the stories in this book, I knew Roz was right in her belief that we had a duty to reprint this book. There is so much richness, so much history, and so much determination in each story.

Today, as the mother to four young Deaf children, I have hopes that my children—who have never known a world without captions, video relay services, interpreters, or the Internet—will appreciate the stories in this book.

Join me as we travel back in time with this book, and marvel at how, no matter the generation, we Deaf people share the time-tested traits of resilience and determination, mixed with a healthy dose of humor.

Trudy Suggs
Savory Words Publishing
June 2018

FOREWORD

A Handful of Stories (1979) was based on the Deaf Storytellers Videotape Series, coordinated by Dr. Roslyn Rosen and Bernard Bragg. They were the guiding forces behind the transliteration of the signed stories into written stories. Mr. Bragg was responsible for recruiting the sixteen deaf individuals for the first volume, and also served as the video tape coordinator.

Another Handful of Stories (1983) was the second volume in the Deaf Storytellers Videotape Series. Dr. Roslyn Rosen and Barbara Kannapell were the guiding forces behind the transliteration of this second set of signed stories. Ms. Kannapell recruited the twenty-four deaf individuals, and also served as the videotape coordinator.

One basic objective of the series was to promote an appreciation of deaf heritage. Thus, the signed and printed stories were based on the personal experiences of the storytellers or on information told to them by other deaf people. Viewers and readers of the stories will find them interesting, informative, sometimes incredible, occasionally moving, and often amusing.

The seventy-four stories included in the series are edited versions of the stories on the videos. They are not transliterations of the signed stories. The videos and the book may be used together, or they may be used independently.

Administrators, teachers, other professionals in educational and other types of institutions, deaf adults, and parents of deaf children will find a variety of uses for the stories, whether in print or on video. People of all ages may view them for entertainment and enjoyment. Students may look at certain stories to obtain bits of historical information. Teachers may incorporate the videos as part of the course of instruction for sign language, English language, or reading classes.

The book may also be used for several other purposes, such as creating interest, arousing curiosity, prompting thinking, or providing vicarious experiences for the readers. The stories can provide an excellent opportunity to encourage recreational reading. With some creativity and effort on the part of a teacher, parent, or leader, lists of words and their meanings can be prepared for some or all of the stories to build vocabulary. Questions and other types of exercises can be designed to develop understanding of the plot, important facts, and the moral of each story. Ideas or facts in the stories can be used as the basis for discussions to expand, reinforce, or review concepts. Some specific suggestions for follow-up activities are included at the end of the book.

Although the videos and the book can be useful learning tools, it was the hope of those who participated in this series that one of the greatest benefits derived from the stories would be that of sheer enjoyment!

To view the storytellers' videos as originally presented, visit www.savorywords.com/ahandfulofstories.

Publisher's note: All contents in this book have been published as they were in the original versions, with edits for clarity or updated terminology.

CHAPTER 1

My First Summer Job

Bernard Bragg

There is a story I would like to share with you. I remember it well, so well that it seems like it happened yesterday. Really, it happened many years ago when I was a young student at Gallaudet College.

I went home to New York for the summer after my first year in college. I spent the whole month of June looking for a job. It was difficult to get a job because so many young people were looking for work. It was a frustrating experience for me. Every time I went into an office and applied for a job, I was told, "No. Sorry, we don't have any openings."

One morning I noticed an advertisement in the newspaper for a dishwasher at a summer camp. I read the ad and thought, "That's fine. I can be a dishwasher." I was excited as I went to the office on 42nd Street near Fifth Avenue. I found that I was the first applicant to arrive. I filled out the application form and then waited. Finally, the secretary told me I could go in for an interview. I went in and found a man standing there. It was obvious that he was the boss. I handed him my application form. He read through it and then started to talk to me.

I had to explain to him that I was deaf. I said, "Wait, I can't hear; please talk slowly." He looked at me and said, "What?" I told him again I was deaf, and he said, "Oh." He pointed to a door and told me to go through the door. I followed his instructions. I opened the door and walked through it, closing it behind me. I found that I was in the hallway near the elevator where I had just come up. I was shocked! He had rejected me without any explanation. I got into the elevator and it descended, I felt very let down. I couldn't understand why he didn't give me a chance to explain that I could do the job well. It didn't require hearing!

I went outside. There were a lot of people passing by on the sidewalk, hurrying along, bumping into me as they walked. The hot sun made me sweat as I walked along. After walking a few steps, I stopped. I thought, "If I give up this easily, I don't think I can go very far in life. I'd better go back and try again." I turned around and went back into the building. I wrote some notes as I rode the elevator. The notes were for the boss. When I walked in, the secretary tried to stop me, but I went right on, walked in, and gave the notes to the boss. He took them and pointed to the door. I told him I wouldn't leave until he read the notes. He looked at me with exasperation, and then started glancing through my notes. He became interested in what I had written. I had explained that I was a student at Gallaudet College, that I needed a job, and that dishwashing didn't require hearing. As he could see, I had arms and they were strong. He kept on reading; he seemed surprised that I could write. Finally, he asked me to have a seat. I sat down, and he asked if I could lipread. I told him I could a little. We talked awhile, and I got the job.

I'll never forget the day I arrived at the summer camp in Massachusetts. It was a beautiful place, set in a clearing surrounded by trees. The scene was exhilarating, but I had to go in and start washing a stack of dirty dishes. (To tell the truth, I hate to wash dishes, but I had to earn a living.) For the next month, I worked like a horse as a dishwasher. But relief finally came.

One day the camp director asked for volunteers to help a nearby farmer with hay gathering. I volunteered because I wanted to get away from the kitchen. Early the next morning, I joined the group of farmers and started pitching hay on a wagon. I worked very hard that morning, so hard that I had blisters all over my hands. My hands were really sore, but I kept on pitching hay until it was time for lunch.

After lunch I was tired, so I decided to lie down under a tree and rest. When I woke up, I found myself all alone. Everyone had gone back to work. I was late! I ran, got my pitchfork, and rushed to the wagon. The foreman was standing on top of the hay. He looked at me with his hands stretched out, nodding his head up and down. Then he put his hands over his ears and stuck out his tongue at me. I was stunned. My first thought was to turn around and walk away, but I decided to stay and keep working. I began pitching hay onto the wagon again.

The hay piled up on the wagon as we moved down the field. It got higher and higher. At the same time black clouds began appearing all around us. It looked like it was it was going to rain at any moment. We hurried to get all the hay we could on the wagon, take it to the barn, and put it in the barn before the rain came. We worked like crazy.

When we got to the barn, the foreman excused everyone except one of the farmers and me. He told me to go up in the loft and spread the hay out while the two of them pitched it up into the loft. The two men pitched the hay in so fast that I couldn't spread it out fast enough. Dust swirled around me; I could hardly breathe; I started coughing; but they kept pitching the hay, and I kept spreading it. I could see that the foreman enjoyed making things hard for me. However, I knew that I could not last much longer. Just as I was about to give up, the foreman looked at me and said, "All right, you can change places with me." He went up in the loft, and I stepped outside. The cold air brushed against my face, and I felt refreshed again. I picked up the pitchfork; now it was my turn. I began to pitch hay into the loft faster than he could spread it. He soon became surrounded by hay, but I kept on working until all the hay was in the loft.

Just then lightning flashed, thunder rolled, and the rain poured down. I staggered off the platform and hit the ground. Rain splattered me as I lay there and rested. After a few minutes I got up, wiped the rain off my face, and began to leave. I noticed the foreman standing under the eaves of the barn, smoking. He nodded his head, indicating he wanted me to come over. I went to him, and he put his hand on my shoulder. I felt as if I had been made a knight—it was like he had tapped me on the shoulder with a sword. I saluted and then turned and walked away.

Trapped!

Deborah M. Sonnenstrahl

When I was a student at George Washington University, in Washington, D.C., I took a course on American Art. One day my teacher gave us some homework. He wanted us to do research on previous artistic styles. My topic was silent movies up until 1929. My teacher wanted me to focus on these movies; they had captions, but no soundtrack. I suspected he did this because I was deaf.

I began looking for information, but I couldn't find anything. I went to my teacher and asked, "Where can I find some good materials for my research?" He suggested that I go to the John F. Kennedy Center for the Performing Arts. He told me that the American Film Institute, located in the Kennedy Center, had an excellent library. I would find a lot of information there about the history of the movies.

I walked into the Kennedy Center one day and asked the woman at the desk where I could find the American Film Institute.

She said, "Go around that corner, and you will see an elevator. Take the elevator to the third floor. You will find the films, books, and papers there."

I thanked her and walked to the elevator. I was so excited I could hardly wait to begin my research. I rang the bell for the elevator and waited. Finally the door opened and I walked in. I was alone in the elevator.

For some strange reason I got a funny feeling; I did not know why. I had never been afraid to be in elevators before, but that time I was. I pushed the funny feeling aside and said to myself, "Debbie, just be cool." The elevator went up and stopped on the third floor, but the door did not open. I started to perspire, and my heart started pounding faster and faster. I pushed the third floor button; I pushed it again and again, but nothing happened! I tried to pry the door open, but I couldn't. I used all my strength, but nothing happened, nothing at all. Then, I thought of pushing the button for another floor. I pressed a button and the elevator went down. The door opened on the first floor, and I ran out. I yelled for the woman at the desk. I cried, "The door wouldn't open on the third floor. The elevator door was shut and I couldn't open it. I couldn't do anything."

The woman looked at me. She said, "But lady, the door on the third floor opens in the back of you."

"In the back of me? You mean on the other side?" I asked.

"Yes," she said, "on the other side."

Oh, just imagine it! How many people must have looked in from the other side and seen me!

The Eavesdropper

Jack R. Gannon

I work in the Alumni Office at Gallaudet College in Washington, D.C. One day I needed to call Bernard Bragg, a deaf actor, at the National Theatre of the Deaf in Connecticut. I asked my secretary to please call him. We have a good telephone interpreting system in our office. I pick up the phone and talk into it, and the secretary listens and tells me what the other person says. It works fine.

That day we called and got the National Theatre. I spoke with a woman saying, "Hello. My name is Jack Gannon. I would like to talk with Mr. Bernard Bragg, please."

The woman said, "Oh, I'm sorry, but Mr. Bragg is deaf."

I was surprised because I thought the National Theatre would have an interpreter for him. "Oh, that's all right," I said, "I'm deaf, too."

"What?" the woman said. "You're deaf. But . . . but . . . you understand me?"

I replied, "Yes, sure, I'm following every word you are saying."

Wondering, she asked, "How?"

I answered, "Oh, I have an eavesdropper next to me."

And she said, "Ohhh . . ."

POW!

Michael Schwartz

When I was a small boy, I went to summer camp every year. One summer I went with my older brother who was about nine years old. We were with a group of hearing boys from New York City. All of them were tough kids from Harlem and the Lower East Side. They played rough with me and with each other.

One of the boys was named Jon. I remember him well. Jon looked exactly like one of the characters on the TV show "The Addams Family." He had a short haircut and curled-up nostrils. For some reason, I didn't feel good about him. One day Jon came to me and moved his mouth like he was talking. I didn't know sign language at that time; I was oral. I looked at him and asked, "What did you say?" He just moved his mouth the same way. Then, I realized he was making fun of me, of the way I talked. I became embarrassed and flustered. I didn't know what to do, so I walked away.

The same thing happened everyday. Jon would come to me and make that same mouth movement. It embarrassed me, but it also made me angry. I felt . . . well, I didn't know how to feel. I decided to find my brother. He was older and wiser, perhaps he would know what to do. I found my brother and told him about Jon. I asked him how I could make Jon stop embarrassing me in front of other people at the camp. I was crying a little bit because I was so upset. I didn't know what to do. My brother looked at me. He made one gesture and said, "Punch him." My brother was busy, he couldn't talk with me, so he just gave me that one line—"punch him"—and left.

I thought, "Punch Jon? I couldn't do that. I couldn't hit another person." I didn't like to fight, and besides I was afraid. But I remembered my brother's one line, "Punch him." One day I went in to my bunk, my bed happened to be right next to Jon's bed. No one else was there, so I went in and got a book. When I turned around, Jon was behind me. He was doing the same thing, making fun of me! I looked at him and then punched him! I hit him right in the mouth. It happened so fast that I didn't know what I was doing. Jon hit the floor; he was out cold. I thought, "My God, what have I done?"

I looked at Jon and he was shaking. Then he began waking up. He looked up at me and was so scared that he took off. I put my book under my arm and walked outside. I was shaking by that time, but I had a good feeling inside of me. It was a beautiful day, and I enjoyed myself, walking around the camp. About an hour, I saw Jon again. I didn't want to fight him, but I didn't have to. When he saw me, he took off again. He didn't want to get close to me. From that day on, I walked very proudly!

My Horse and I

Mary Beth Miller

When I was a very young girl, I liked to sit and dream and imagine things. One day I fantasized that I had a horse. He was black with a white spot on his forehead. The spot looked like a star. He was a beautiful, big horse, and how he could gallop! I thought about my horse often. I talked to him, played with him, petted him, and rode him. I loved my horse, he was smart. He could jump far without hurting himself. The horse of my fantasy was very real.

One day I went to visit my mother's friend. (She is deaf, too.) I told her, "I have a horse at home. He eats grass. He is black with a white star on his forehead. Last night I rode and rode him."

My mother's friend said, "How nice."

The next week I went to visit her again. I told her some more about my black horse with the white star. I told her how the horse jumped and how I rode him all over the farm.

My friend said, "How nice."

Every week I would tell my friend different stories about my horse. But finally, my stories ran out. My mind was blank; I didn't know what to do. One day I said to her, "I don't have my horse anymore. He died."

"Your horse died!" she said. "What happened?"

"Oh, my uncle shot him," I answered. "It was my uncle's fault."

My friend felt bad, but she wasn't really sure about my story. Later, when I wasn't around, she went to my house, knocked on the door, and said to my mother, "Do you have a horse, a black horse with a white star on his forehead?"

"What are you talking about?" my mother asked. "We don't have a horse here. The city doesn't allow horses; it is against the law."

My friend, puzzled and wondering, went home.

The next day, I went to my friend's house again. "I buried my horse," I told her. "I put a cross on the grave. I prayed and I cried."

My friend said, "Are you telling me the truth?"

"Yes," I replied, "I'm telling you the truth."

"No, you are not," she said. "I asked your mother, and she said there's no black horse with a white star. She was surprised. You are telling me a lie."

"I wasn't telling you a lie. I was only fantasizing, but my horse seemed real to me."

CHAPTER 2

Spaced Out!

Jerald M. Jordan

I would like to tell you a story about a deaf man and some experiments with weightlessness and motion sickness. The man was not Superman, but perhaps we could call him Super J.J. I am that man.

Early in the 1960s, a group of U.S. Navy doctors were looking for a cure for motion sickness. They wanted to prevent people from becoming sick while they were on boats or while they were weightless in space. A lot of people have a tendency to become ill and throw up when they are on a boat or roller coaster. Many hearing people have this problem, and many deaf people have it, too. I don't because when I was seven years old, I had spinal meningitis. That disease destroyed my hearing and my sense of balance. From that time on, I have had no sense of balance, and I have to depend on my vision for balance. If I stand on one leg, I can balance fine; but if I close my eyes, I fall down.

The doctors knew that I had no sense of balance, and they wanted to compare me with people who get motion sickness. A few other deaf people and I went to a naval base in Florida for some experiments. Many of the experiments were the same as the ones they did on the astronauts before they went into space. The doctors were hoping to lessen the effect of weightlessness on hearing people. Some of the experiments were really boring, but some of them were exciting. The most exciting experiment of all took place in a large four-engine airplane. Inside, there were no seats; everything had been taken out and soft padding had been used to cover the inside of the plane. In the weightless experiment if someone hit the padded wall, ceiling, or floor of the airplane, the person wasn't injured. The doctors took movies and pictures so they could study what happened.

When the plane was in the air, it started out flying level; then it went up into an arch. While the plane was in the arch, we deaf people were weightless for about forty-five seconds. We were very heavy for a brief time, but then we began to have no weight. All we needed to do was touch something and we floated. We rolled over, forward, backward, to the side—everywhere in the air—with no support. We couldn't push against or touch anything hard because we would hit the wall and bounce back and forth. It was difficult to stop; someone had to catch us and stop us from bouncing. It is hard to describe exactly how I felt during that experiment, but it was wonderful.

One of the hearing doctors with us was a short man who weighed about 250 pounds. Once when we were weightless, I picked him up! I tossed him through the air like a football to another person who caught him and threw him back to me. It was easy, and the doctor was a good sport!

However, every good thing ends. When the plane came down from the arch, we felt that we weighed more than twice our normal weight. That was because of the pull of gravity. At the time of the experiments I was rather fat; I weighed about 190 pounds. At two-and-a-half times my weight, I felt that I weighed about 500 pounds. After a while, I felt my normal weight again. Then the cycle was repeated—flying level, going up into an arch, and coming down from the arch. During each arch of the plane, we became weightless and floated in the plane.

Some of the hearing people didn't like the experiments. Once we went up with a group of hearing sailors. A few of them were navy pilots who had flown jets for many years. When we took off and became weightless, one of the sailors thought it was easy. But he soon got sick and began vomiting. He became so sick that the doctor on the plane had to help him. The sailor was cold and shaking. Because of this, the pilot had to dump most of the fuel to lighten the plane and then land. The sick sailor was taken to the hospital. It was strange that he, a hearing person, got sick, but I never did. I had a good time with the experiments.

Another interesting experience was when a group of hearing sailors and a group of deaf people went to Nova Scotia. We were there in February, and that is one of the worst places in the world in the winter. It was extremely cold, we had to wear warm clothes—hats, mittens, the works. Usually the water off Nova Scotia is very rough, but the day we were to board the ship to begin our experiment, the water was calm. The navy people weren't too happy because they wanted rough water. We waited three days for some bad weather, but there was none. Finally, on the fourth day a storm hit. It was so bad that three ships went down in the ocean that day. We were told to hurry and get ready to board the ship.

Before we left the calm water in the harbor, the doctors took a blood sample from each person in the experiment. They wanted to do that every hour so they could analyze what happened to the body and how it changed while we were on the rough water. After the doctors took blood samples we sailed out into the ocean, and the full force of the storm hit us! The water was rough and the waves were high— thirty to thirty-five feet high! The ship went up and down, and I tell you, I was scared. I couldn't walk; I had to crawl on all fours. After about an hour of this, though, I lost my fear and became rather confident that the ship wouldn't sink.

The doctors wanted to take blood every hour, so after the first hour I went to one of their offices. There the doctor was, laid out sick. I went to another doctor, and found the same thing. All the doctors were so ill they couldn't conduct their experiment. The hearing sailors were sick, too. The six of us who were deaf and one hearing person were the only ones not in bed. We sat around a table playing cards; there was nothing else to do. It was dark outside, and the ocean was rough. I looked at the hearing person and said, "You're not sick?"

"No, I feel fine," he answered.

"Why aren't you sick?" I asked him. "Everyone else is sick."

"He replied, "I have spent thirty-five years on a U.S. destroyer. Destroyers are rather small ships which are easily tossed about."

We continued playing cards. About fifteen minutes later I looked and the hearing man was gone, too. That left only the deaf people, plus, thank God, the captain of the ship and his crew. They had sailed these waters for many years and the rough seas didn't bother them.

The crew members were French. They were hearing people, but they didn't speak English. That night, while we were playing cards, the captain came to the table. He looked at us and gestured to ask if we were sick. We gestured back that we were fine. He couldn't believe it. We continued playing cards all night; we couldn't sleep because we would have fallen out of bed. From time to time the captain came in and asked us if we were ill. He seemed almost disappointed when we answered that we were not. I didn't understand why he seemed disappointed. Later I found out that the admiral, a navy doctor who was responsible for the experiment, had made a bet with the captain. He bet a case of Scotch whiskey that we would not get sick. That was why the captain hoped to see us sick, but he lost the bet!

So you see, that is how some deaf people helped our astronauts before they ever went to the moon. Without our help, maybe they would never have gotten there because of problems with weightlessness and motion sickness. Thank goodness for the help of some deaf people in getting the astronauts to the moon!

Gallaudet Theatre on Broadway

Eric Malzkuhn

I would like to take you back in the past—back to a time when my waist was smaller and I had a lot more hair. That was in the 1940s when I was a student at Gallaudet College. I was fascinated with the theatre and wanted to become involved in it. Naturally, I volunteered to act. My first "role" in a play was as the curtain-puller. That was all I did. However, I began to get some acting roles after that.

The summer I was a sophomore I read many different plays. I was looking for a good play for Gallaudet to put on the next year. I wanted something better than Samuel French's *Blue Plate Special*. I wanted something new, something exciting, so I read and read. Then something hit me! *Arsenic and Old Lace* was the play I wanted! I knew it was being acted on Broadway at the time. I was young and inexperienced so I was not afraid to write and ask to see if we could get the play. I sent a letter to the Dramatist Play Service, which controlled the rights to *Arsenic and Old Lace*. I received a letter saying that they were sorry, but the play was not available for amateurs until the end of the New York run. Also, it was not available to professional groups without an agreement about money and other matters. I was heartbroken, but I wasn't satisfied either. I wrote another letter, a longer one, explaining that the Gallaudet students were not professionals, but they were not amateurs, either. I told them that all the money earned was put into the treasury for costumes, sets, and similar things for play productions. I also said that we were the best sign language actors in the world! I sent the letter. I waited one week, but there was no response. I started to get depressed. Then one morning word came to me that there was a box downstairs for me. A box? I went down and found a box from New York for me. My eyes opened wide, and my heart began beating fast as I looked in the box. There were twenty-one scripts of *Arsenic and Old Lace* and a note. The note said, "Is this what you wanted?" It was signed by Howard Lindsay and Russell Crouse. Maybe those names are not familiar now, but they were famous people in 1940. They wrote *Life with Father*, and they produced *Arsenic and Old Lace*.

When I got the box, the Gallaudet actors were ready to do the play on the small stage in Chapel Hall. We were satisfied with that. I was to direct the play—oh, I was so excited. Our group met and began to make plans. While we were planning, a boy came and said there was a telegram for me. "Who would send me a telegram?" I wondered. I got it, opened it, and read, "Why not forget about presenting *Arsenic and Old Lace* in Chapel Hall? Why not do it at the National Theatre in downtown Washington?" Wow! I couldn't believe it. Then I noticed that the telegram said in March. Our rehearsal time wouldn't be long enough if we did it in March. May was the best time; March was too soon.

I didn't know what to do, but before I had a chance to do anything, another telegram came. I opened it. "Forget the first telegram," it read. "We realize we were pushing you. Plan on performing the play on Broadway in May."

I was floating on air! I decided I couldn't direct the play; I was only nineteen. I had better give the job to someone wiser and more skilled than I. I ran to Dr. Hughes and asked him, "Would you like to direct our play?"

"Well," he said, "I am rather busy right now."

"How would you like to take our play to Broadway?" I asked.

"Broadway!" he said as his eyes popped out.

I explained, and he accepted the offer. We shook hands on it.

We got a letter two or three days later from the Broadway producers. "We would appreciate it if you and Dr. Hughes would come to New York, watch our play, meet our actors, and talk about various plans," they wrote. Lindsay and Crouse thought this visit would be important for publicity for Gallaudet College and also for their play. So we went to New York. They made hotel reservations for us and told us just to sign for our meals at the hotel. This was a new experience in my life! The first time we went to eat, I ordered lots of things. After the meal, I very nonchalantly asked for the check and signed my name. The waiter looked at it. He looked at the name and then looked at me. He had never heard of Eric Malzkuhn. The waiter went to phone about the check while I sat there. When he came back, he was all smiles. Everything was fine.

That night we went to the Fulton Theatre, now called the Helen Hayes Theatre, and saw the play *Arsenic and Old Lace* for the first time. We sat in the third row of the center section. The curtain opened and Boris Karloff, the star, came on stage. Chills ran up and down my spine. Karloff is the famous actor who played Frankenstein in the movies. I'll never forget that moment; it was very exciting. During intermission, at the end of the first act, Russell Crouse came down the aisle and waved to us. He asked, "Is everything all right?"

"Fine," we replied. People looked at us wondering who we were. My buttons were popping, but I couldn't help it, I felt so proud. When the play was finished, we met Boris Karloff. He was very pleasant, very nice. He shook my hand. "I am happy to have you come here," he said. "You can use my costume and my shoes." That night we met in the hotel and talked business.

When it was time to order drinks, they asked me if I wanted a drink. "Well," I thought, "I'm not in college right now." Drinking was forbidden at Gallaudet, but I was in New York. So I decided I would have an old-fashioned. Then they asked Dr. Hughes.

He looked at me and said, "I'll just have some milk, please."

Lindsay said, "Oh, no. Malz won't tell on you."

"Okay," said Dr. Hughes, "I'll have a whiskey sour."

We were really stuck on one point. We hadn't gotten approval from the Gallaudet administration to do the play in New York. Imagine, if you can, that we had to go to the president of Gallaudet and ask him to let us know within three days if our group could go to New York to do *Arsenic and Old Lace*. We met with President Hall and explained the whole thing. Dr. Hall, a man I loved very dearly, said, "No. I am sorry, but you can't. I am rejecting the idea."

We were heartbroken. He never explained his reason. Perhaps he feared that the deaf being linked with Frankenstein (Karloff) would create some sort of monster-image on people's minds. Or possibly he didn't want to change the play into a silent one. I don't know his reason, but he turned it down.

We thought about it and tried to decide what we could do. Then Jon Hall, the president's son, said, "Ask the faculty for a vote." Jon was a very good friend of ours. He worked hard for us; he helped us a lot with the sets. We went to the faculty and they voted that we should do the play on Broadway.

We did it! We went to New York and we were a big hit. It was fantastic! Dr. Hall admitted in front of a national audience that he was wrong. The play, which was also filmed, was a great success. We were in New York for five days. We stayed at a hotel and signed for our meals like Dr. Hughes and I had done before. We rehearsed all day, but at night we went to see plays. We saw Gertrude Lawrence,

Victor Mature, and Danny Kaye in *Lady in the Dark* and Theresa Wright in *Life with Father*. It was magnificent, marvelous.

Once a newspaper man came in and asked for a picture of me scaring Karloff. Can you imagine me scaring him? I tried and the man took the picture of me with my features frozen in a grimace, trying to scare Boris Karloff!

During the time we were rehearsing the play, I wore Boris Karloff's costume. I wore it when I was out walking, and when I went out for lunch. I even wore his shoes. He called them his lucky shoes because he wore them inside his boots when playing the part of Frankenstein. When I first tried the shoes on, he asked if they fit. They were too big, but I said they were fine. I put some paper in the toes of the shoes.

On May 10, 1942, the curtain opened on *Arsenic and Old Lace* performed by Gallaudet students on Broadway. One man, a rather famous deaf priest, was sitting on the aisle. He told me he was afraid that deaf people gesturing and signing would be too much like overacting and people would laugh at us. He sat on the aisle so he could leave quickly. Well, he didn't leave. He sat in rapt attention, just as the critics did. Afterward the priest said it was marvelous. Burns Mantle, probably the most famous New York critic at the time, said that he thought Gallaudet students should come back to New York every year. That did not happen, but that is another story.

Those moments were some of the most beautiful of my life. Of course, being on Broadway, I became very conceited. When I went back to Gallaudet, I still had a big head. I was strutting about, and Elizabeth Peet, one of our professors, came up to me and said, "Mr. Malzkuhn, it was a wonderful, wonderful play. But your French is not so wonderful." That helped reduce my swelled head and got me back to normal again!

Man's Best Friend

J. Matt Searls

A long time ago two boys lived in the country near a small town. One boy's name was John. The other boy, who lived a few houses down the lane, was named Mark. John and Mark were the best of friends.

One day John and Mark had been playing. When they got tired, Mark said, "Maybe we could walk into town." John said he really didn't want to do that. "What else do we have to do?" asked Mark. "Maybe we can buy some candy and look around." So John agreed to go.

As they walked toward town, they noticed a man putting up a sign. John and Mark were curious, so they watched the man until he finished, and then they walked over and read the sign. It said that a circus was coming to town the next week. John said, "Maybe we can go to the circus." Mark agreed it was a good idea, but they didn't have any money.

They saw on the sign that a ticket to get into the circus would be one dollar. Where could they get the money? Mark had an idea. He said, "We could sell lemonade this week for five cents a glass and earn a dollar each. Then we could buy our tickets for the circus." John thought that was a good idea. All that week the two of them sold lemonade to the passersby at five cents a drink. They worked hard in the hot sun. As the time drew near for the circus to open, they counted their money. They counted out two dollars for the tickets, but there was some money left. They counted it and found there was another dollar. They had earned three dollars altogether. John suggested that they use the extra money to buy popcorn, cotton candy, and other things like that at the circus. So they divided the dollar, fifty cents each, and waited for the circus to open.

That morning, John got up, dressed quickly, ate no breakfast, and took off to Mark's house. When Mark was ready, the boys left his house. In the distance they saw the Big Top. They ran toward the tent, and soon there it was before them—the Big Top!

The boys looked around; they had never seen anything like the circus. They bought their tickets and went inside. When they got inside, they saw the trapeze, the high wire, the bright colors, and the beautiful lights. They saw the animals—elephants, lions, dogs, and other animals. John said that the circus was going to be exciting. They bought some candy and then looked for a seat right down in front. They sat down and soon the ringmaster came in. Then the circus began. One act was the lion tamer and the lions. When that was over, the bears, elephants, horses, and other animals performed. Then it was time for the man on the high wire. Mark was excited, but John was nervous; he was afraid to watch the high wire act. Mark thought John was chicken. After that the dogs came out—big dogs, fat dogs, cute little dogs with bows, many kinds of dogs. John was fascinated. The dogs jumped up, they sat, they lay down, and they rolled over. Too soon the circus was over, but both boys had enjoyed it.

On the way home Mark asked John, "What act did you enjoy the most?"

John said, "I liked the dogs; they were so intelligent."

"I liked the man on the high wire," Mark said. "That took some courage."

As they walked along, John thought he noticed something across the road. He asked Mark if he saw something, but Mark said that he didn't see anything. John suggested that they check it out. They did and found a cute brown puppy with a white spot on his forehead. He was cold and cowering, and his ears were drooping. John thought the puppy looked afraid. What should they do? Should they leave the puppy there or take him home? John decided to take him home. Mark thought it was better to leave him there. If the puppy was lost, his mother might find him. But John felt that if the puppy were left, he might die of hunger.

John picked up the little dog and said good-bye to Mark. When John got home, he knocked on the door. His mother opened the door and saw the puppy he was holding. She said, "You put that dog back." John told his mother that the little dog was hungry and cold. With his droopy ears, the puppy looked so sad. John's mother said, "You can bring him in, but if you do, you have to bathe and feed him. Tomorrow you must put an ad in the newspaper about the little dog. Maybe someone owns him."

John was a little depressed about the ad, but he agreed. He went to the newspapers the next day and explained to them how he found the puppy. There were advertisements in the paper for a week trying to find the owner. All that week John took care of the little dog. What a change! The puppy became quite healthy; his eyes sparkled and his ears perked up. At the end of the week John had heard nothing. It seemed that no one wanted the dog. John's mother said he could keep the dog. However, John had to promise to feed him properly, take him outside to go to the bathroom, and accept all responsibility for the dog. John agreed.

John had to decide what to name the dog. Since the dog had a white spot on his forehead, maybe his name should be Star. That name didn't sound too good to John. Perhaps Spot would be a good name. That was the name John decided on for his dog. John and Spot became inseparable. John trained the dog to sit, lie down, and roll over.

John spent so much time training Spot that Mark became jealous. Mark said, "John, you are always playing with your dog." John reminded Mark that he had to train Spot and take care of him; it was his responsibility. Mark told John that the two of them were always together before. Now the dog was interfering, and he didn't like it! He suggested that John get rid of Spot. John said, "I love the dog. It can be the three of us; we can all be friends."

Mark replied, "No, the three of us can't be friends. I can't be friends with Spot."

"Wait," said John. "I'll show you." Then he looked at Spot and said, "Friends," and the dog extended his paw to Mark.

But Mark said, "I don't want to touch the dog; he is dirty."

When the time came for John to go to school, his mother said, "John, you have to leave the dog at home. When you come home from school, you can play with him." John was sad; he wanted to take Spot to school. However, John went to school, and then every evening when he came home, he took care of his dog and played with him. John also played with his friend Mark. When the school year ended and summertime came, John and Mark were still friends. Mark continued to feel that Spot was interfering with his and John's relationship. Mark would say to John, "Leave the dog at home and let's go out."

John would always say, "No. He's a good dog; he is our friend."

"He is not my friend," Mark would reply. But John always took Spot with them. The boys went swimming and did different things, but the dog was always with them.

One summer day John and Mark decided they would go swimming in a pond near a big waterfall. They liked going there; they used to swing from a rope tied to a tall tree and jump into the water. As usual, Mark wanted John to leave the dog at home. "Spot can't swim," Mark said. "He can't jump from the rope. Why should he go?"

John said, "Maybe Spot can look around and even go for a swim."

Mark didn't say any more, but he was angry.

The three of them walked to the waterfall and pond. It was a beautiful place. John and Mark jumped from the rope, fell into the pond, swam, and played all afternoon. Meanwhile, Spot sniffed around and watched the two boys. When the boys grew tired, they lay on a rock and enjoyed the hot sun and the cool breeze. Soon John and Mark were asleep.

A little later, Mark woke John up and asked, "Would you like to go for another swim?"

"No," John said, "I'm too tired. I am going to lie here in the sun. You go on for a swim if you want to."

Mark got up to go, but he told John he didn't want Spot to go with him. John told Spot to stay there. Then John fell asleep again; it was very comfortable in the hot sun.

A little while later Spot began to bark. John woke up and saw Spot looking down at the water at the bottom of the waterfall. Mark was down there; he had obviously fallen and was trying to swim. John and Spot ran down the hill. They both jumped in the water, and John pulled Mark to safety. When they were on the bank, the two boys breathed a sigh of relief. John asked what had happened. Mark explained that he had fallen from the rope and sprained his ankle; now it was swollen.

"Mark," John said, "Spot barked and woke me up. It is a good thing that the two of us were here to help you."

Mark replied, "Yes, I guess you are right." He looked at Spot who sat there wagging his tail. Mark said, "Friend," and Spot extended his paw. Mark shook Spot's paw and then put his arm around John. From that day on, John, Mark, and Spot were friends; the three of them were always together.

Have Interpreter, Will Talk

Edward E. Corbett, Jr.

I want to tell you a true story—something funny that really happened to me. When I was working with the United States Congress in Washington, D.C., I worked with the Committee on Education and Labor. One of my duties was to study Section 504 actions on the federal level. The 504 law says that handicapped people will not be discriminated against or prevented from participating in programs or activities that require federal funding. In doing my job, I contacted many different departments such as Health, Education, and Welfare; Defense; Labor; Justice; State; Agriculture; and others.

At the Department of Health, Education, and Welfare (HEW), I wanted to get in touch with someone in the Office of Civil Rights, OCR for short. I wanted to find out from that person what problems OCR had involving Section 504. I needed information about problems such as how many people complained about discrimination under 504, what actions had been taken by that office regarding the complaints, and how the complaints had been or could be resolved.

Through an interpreter I made a phone call, well actually not one, but more than twenty calls, with no success. Finally after two weeks, I talked with a member of Congress. I explained to him that my phone calls had not been returned and that I could not get through to the Office of Civil Rights. He called the Secretary of HEW, who had a secretary call the director of OCR. The director asked someone to call me to set up an appointment so we could get together. Finally the phone call came.

I was at the Maryland School for the Deaf when the call came from the Office of Civil Rights. The man who called said that their office understood I had been trying to set up a meeting at OCR, and they were ready to meet with me. The call came on Thursday, and the gentleman suggested that we get together the following week on Monday, Tuesday, or Wednesday. I said that was fine; Monday would be best for me. We set the meeting for Monday afternoon at two o'clock, and I wrote it on my calendar. Then the man asked me if I would bring along an interpreter. I said, "No! Section 504 says that you should provide me with an interpreter. Why should I always have to look around and find an interpreter to take with me to different meetings? Why should I suffer?" For these reasons I did not agree to bring an interpreter.

"Well," the gentleman said, "perhaps we have a problem."

I agreed, "Yes, we do. Today is Thursday, and we only have Friday, Saturday, Sunday, and Monday to find an interpreter. It is not easy to get an interpreter on such short notice. Sometimes you have to reserve one as much as a month ahead of time.

"But that is okay," I continued. "We can forget about an interpreter because we can still communicate."

"How?" he asked.

"We can write notes."

"That is impossible," the man replied.

I got very angry and said, "I can read and write!"

"No, no, don't misunderstand me," he said. "I said it is impossible because, you see, I am blind. I can't read or communicate through reading."

I started to laugh. I was with the United States Congress, and I wanted to discuss something really important about 504 with someone at the national level. He was blind, and I was deaf! I laughed and laughed, and he laughed and laughed. It was really funny. We postponed the meeting to another time when we could get an interpreter.

Later I related my strange experience to a few members of Congress. They said they didn't realize that interpreters were hard to find. They thought perhaps something should be done to help provide more interpreters. I agreed and said we should come up with a way to set up interpreter training programs. "If we could find some money," I suggested, "we could find many hearing people and could teach them to become interpreters."

The members agreed with me. So, we took that idea and wrote a bill for Congress. That bill became the law which President Carter signed in 1978. It is called the Interpreter Training Act of 1978.

CHAPTER 3

Laurent Clerc: The Greatest Teacher of All Time

Gilbert C. Eastman

June 28, 1864, was an important day for deaf people. On that day, many people gathered in a church in Washington, D.C. The big event was the birth of Gallaudet College. The president of the college was only twenty-nine years old. His name was Edward Miner Gallaudet. He stood up, saw all the people gathered in front of him, and gave his opening inaugural speech. Government officials, members of Congress, ministers, and deaf children from Kendall School were seated on the platform to watch this great celebration.

Several members of Edward M. Gallaudet's family were in the audience, including his sixty-six year old mother, Sophia Fowler Gallaudet, and his oldest brother, Thomas Gallaudet. Thomas and Edward were the sons of Thomas Hopkins Gallaudet, the founder of the first permanent school for the deaf in America. Now Thomas Hopkins Gallaudet's youngest son was helping to establish Gallaudet College. A deaf man was also sitting there, an artist, whose name was John Carlin. He was to receive an honorary degree. Several famous speakers came up to the podium, one by one, and gave long speeches. Then, Edward Miner Gallaudet introduced an old man who was seventy-nine years old. The old man trembled a little and appeared to be weak. When Gallaudet fingerspelled his name, Laurent Clerc got up, walked to the podium, and faced all of the people. The hearing people applauded, and the deaf people waved their handkerchiefs, as was their custom. Clerc looked at Edward Miner Gallaudet, who was so young. He looked at Edward's older brother and at their mother. Even though he was old, Clerc's mind was still very clear and straight, and he began to think back many, many years . . . .

Laurent Clerc was born in France in 1785. Those were terrible times in that country—it was the time of the French Revolution, Bastille

Day, and a reign of terror during which many people, including the king and queen, were beheaded. Blood flowed all over France. It was at that time that Clerc was born.

Clerc was born in LaBalme, a town in the south of France. At the age of two he had an unfortunate accident. He was sitting in a high chair and, somehow, the chair fell over on the hearth. Laurent hit the side of his head. As a result of the fall, he became deaf and he lost his sense of smell. Clerc's sign is made by brushing the first two fingers on the cheek because of the two scares he had on the side of his head.

Young Clerc played with the children in the neighborhood for several years, but when they went to school, he was left alone. He played by himself outside—in the woods, beside the streams, and on the rolling hills—until he was twelve years old. That year his uncle came to visit the family. He saw that Clerc was already twelve years old and had never been to school; he had no formal education. The uncle persuaded Clerc's parents to send him to Paris where they had a school for the deaf. His mother and father hated to send their son so far away from home. However, they permitted his uncle to take him in a stagecoach from LaBalme to Paris.

Clerc's uncle dropped him off at the school; there he met a deaf teacher named Jean Massieu. The superintendent of the school, Abbé Sicard, was not there at the time. Abbé Sicard had been arrested, put into jail, and was waiting to be beheaded. Jean Massieu was so worried about the superintendent that he decided to call the deaf people of Paris together. He wanted to see what they could do to get the Abbé released. The people decided to sign a petition and take it to the French Assembly. There, in front of all the hearing people, Jean Massieu read the letter from the deaf people pleading that Abbé Sicard be released. After several days of consideration the Assembly decided to free the Abbé and let him return to his school, the Paris Institute for the Deaf.

While Clerc was growing up at the school, he became Abbé Sicard's favorite pupil. The Abbé and Massieu both taught Laurent. He proved to be very brilliant even though he hadn't had any schooling until the age of twelve. Later, when Clerc was in his twenties, Abbé

Sicard offered him a teaching position at the Institute in Paris, and he accepted.[1] Clerc taught in the Paris school for many years.

People from other countries visited the school to see Massieu's and Clerc's classes and to study how they taught deaf children. Their techniques began to spread to other countries. A man from St. Petersburg, Russia, came to the school to see Clerc's work. He was impressed and asked Clerc if he would be willing to teach in Russia. Clerc agreed to go; he was excited and eager to teach in a Russian school. The Abbé did not like the idea, but he said it was Clerc's decision. The Russian returned to St. Petersburg to make arrangements. Clerc waited and waited for the Russian to return, but he didn't come back. Finally, Laurent heard from him; he said that they didn't have enough money, so he had to cancel the offer of a teaching job. Clerc was disappointed, but if the man from Russia had found some money and taken Clerc to St. Petersburg to teach, this story would be quite different.

Napoleon had many enemies in France, one of whom was Abbé Sicard. Sicard was afraid of Napoleon, so he decided to go into exile. He took Clerc and Massieu, and they escaped across the channel to London, England. While in England, the three teachers continued their work; they traveled around and gave lectures to the English people. They went to lecture halls where many of the important people gathered. The people asked questions which Sicard interpreted to Clerc and Massieu. The two deaf teachers answered the questions by writing on the blackboard. The hearing people were shocked that deaf people could write.

One day the Duke of Kent, the Duchess of Wellington, and the Duke of Orleans, three very important people in England, were at the lecture. The Duke of Wellington, the Duchess' husband, was leading the English army against Napoleon's troops at Waterloo.

---

[1] *I have a picture of Clerc as a young man in Paris. I found the picture, a very small photograph, in the Library of Congress and had it enlarged. In the picture the front of Clerc's head is bald. As I looked at the picture, I wondered why the front of his head was bald, since later pictures of Clerc show him with a full head of hair. I found the answer to my question. Clerc was a young man during the time of Napoleon, the French emperor. At that time the young men in Paris looked to Napoleon as their fashion guide. Napoleon was balding in the front, so many of the men then shaved the front of their heads. Later on, of course, Clerc let his hair grow in front.*

During the lecture, while the people were asking questions, Sicard was interpreting, and Clerc and Massieu were answering, the Prince Regent came rushing into the lecture hall. "The war is over," he shouted! "We have won at Waterloo, we defeated Napoleon." Napoleon lost, the Duke of Wellington (whose wife was sitting there that day) and his men won, and Massieu and Clerc witnessed that historical event.

Abbé Sicard made plans for Clerc, Massieu, and himself to leave London and go back home. They continued to give lectures up until their last day in England. A short man from America attended their last lecture. The man was very impressed with the lecture and the question and answer session. When the three teachers were finished, the young man from America came to the front and introduced himself to Sicard, Clerc, and Massieu. His name was Thomas Hopkins Gallaudet. Gallaudet shook hands with the three men and then explained that he wanted to establish a school for the deaf in America. Sicard invited Gallaudet to go to Paris and visit his school; however, Gallaudet wanted to spend a few more days in England. He traveled around, observing the various methods of teaching deaf children used in English schools. Gallaudet became quite frustrated with what he saw. After he finished his travels in England, he went to Paris to learn the art of teaching the deaf. He studied Massieu's and Clerc's classes for several months.

Meanwhile, the people in Hartford, Connecticut, who had sent Gallaudet to Europe, were saying to him, "Come home. You have stayed too long." Gallaudet realized it was time to leave, so he told Clerc, "I have to go back to America. Could you find two deaf teachers for me who are skilled both in English and French?" Clerc said he would be happy to help. He found two deaf teachers and presented their names to Gallaudet.

Gallaudet looked at the names and changed his mind. He said to Clerc, "I don't want these men; I want you."

"You want me?" Clerc replied. "But, I don't know English."

Gallaudet said, "You can learn English."

Suddenly Clerc became excited about the idea of going to America. Gallaudet offered him a three-year contract and Clerc accepted. Of course, Sicard became very upset; he didn't want Clerc to leave Paris. The deaf children there needed him. Massieu didn't want him to go; he thought it was a stupid idea. But Clerc was stubborn and decided to go anyway.

Before leaving for America, Clerc wanted to go home to visit his mother and the rest of his family. Clerc's mother had already heard the news and she was upset. She asked, "Why are you going to America?"

"I must," Clerc said. "I must help the deaf children in America. They have no teachers. There are no hearing or deaf teachers in America."

His mother tried to persuade him to stay in France, but Clerc remained firm. After two weeks his family finally gave up and wished him good-bye. He took a stagecoach back to Paris. The day after he arrived in Paris he went to the office and signed his three-year contract. Everything was ready. He packed his suitcase and went by coach to Le Havre to board a ship. Clerc stood on the dock and looked out across the sea. What was ahead of him was unknown, but he mustered up his courage and got on the ship.

Traveling by ship from France to America in those days took fifty-two days. Gallaudet and Clerc used their time wisely during the trip. Gallaudet taught Clerc English, and Clerc taught Gallaudet sign language. You might think the trip was a pleasant one, but it was not. They encountered terrible storms at sea. People got sick, and many passengers had to stay in bed. Clerc suffered a lot during the trip. Sometimes the sea was calm, so the ship remained under the hot sun for several days. The room where Clerc stayed would get very, very hot, and he would perspire. When the weather changed, the room would get very, very cold, so Clerc would pile on the blankets. But Gallaudet continued studying sign language, and Clerc continued studying English until they reached New York.

When the ship arrived in New York, Clerc looked around the city. New York City didn't look like it does today! Clerc didn't like the looks of the buildings. The city seemed very plain and humble compared to Paris which had fancy buildings, museums, and theaters. Clerc became homesick for Paris; he wanted to go back, even after the long trip. But he agreed to go on with Gallaudet, so they traveled by stagecoach to Hartford. Clerc again became upset because the people there all dressed the same.

Gallaudet and Clerc went to the Cogswell house in Hartford. They met Mrs. Cogswell, who immediately asked someone to go call her daughter Alice. The two men talked with Mrs. Cogswell while they wanted for Alice. Clerc was still disappointed with America and kept saying he wanted to go home. Gallaudet, who was interpreting for Clerc, was heartbroken that the teacher did not like America. Finally Alice Cogswell, who was deaf, came in and met Clerc. She began to gesture and sign to him. Clerc was shocked! Alice already knew some sign language. She used some gestures, but she also used signs. Clerc wondered how she knew them. He asked and found out that Gallaudet had been teaching Alice before he decided to go to Europe. Since Gallaudet didn't want to leave Alice at home without a teacher, he put her in a private school for girls. The teacher at the school, Lydia Huntley, taught Alice and all the hearing girls in the class to use signs so Alice and the other girls could communicate. Thanks to Lydia Huntley, the girls developed their own sign language. When Clerc saw this, he thought it was wonderful. Alice and Clerc became very close.

Gallaudet wanted to establish a school for the Deaf in Hartford. He worked for one year to raise money. Then he established his school, not in a school building, but in a hotel.[2] The school took over the first, second, and third floors of the hotel. The classrooms were on the first floor and the sleeping quarters on the second and third floors. When the school opened, there were seven deaf pupils; one of them was Alice Cogswell. The school stayed in the hotel for a year until Gallaudet, with the help of some businessmen, found another place, a big house. They moved into the house, and it became the

---

[2] *I have a picture of that hotel. While I was doing my research, I knew that the American School for the Deaf had a picture of three of the early buildings, but they had no picture of the original building. I looked around and by accident, I found a very tiny picture. The name on it was City Hotel; I had heard that name before. I learned that the City Hotel was the exact place where Gallaudet and Clerc established the first school. I was so excited. I took the picture to a photographer and had it enlarged.*

first real school building, although it was the second building for the school.

Clerc taught the seven students in the school. The two oldest pupils were Elizabeth Boardman and Sophia Fowler. These two girls were between seventeen and nineteen years old. The other students were about fourteen. For two years, while Clerc taught, he kept noticing Elizabeth. Gradually he fell in love with her. He proposed marriage to her, and they were married after she finished school. After the birth of their first baby, Clerc decided to go to Philadelphia with his family. The school there needed some help. Clerc helped the school make some changes to improve its program. He also taught in the school for a time. While the Clerc family was in Philadelphia, Clerc heard that the famous American painter, William Peale, lived in the city. Clerc asked the painter if he would paint a portrait of the Clerc family. Mr. Peale agreed, and he painted two pictures of them.

After seven months in Philadelphia, Clerc and his family moved back to Hartford. The family gradually grew larger. Laurent and Elizabeth had six children, four girls and two boys. Two children died at birth. The oldest daughter became a teacher at the school for the deaf, the second child became a minister, their other daughter married the mayor of Hartford, and their youngest son studied the silk business in France. After several years he came back to the United States and established his own business in New York City.

As Gallaudet and Clerc worked together, their friendship grew even stronger. Together they taught, raised money, and conducted experiments. Some of their experiments were strange! Gallaudet was not satisfied with the manual alphabet. He was still a strong oralist and was not happy with fingerspelling. He invented a new alphabet—the alphabet of scents. (That is puzzling, isn't it?) He took twenty-six jars and put a different substance in each jar. Each substance had a strong odor. For instance, *A* was ammonia; *B* was bergamot, which smells almost like mint; *C* was cinnamon; and so forth. Gallaudet put the twenty-six different scents on one side of a wall. A student would like a stick, dip it in the jar, and wave it over the top of the wall. Students on the other side of the wall would smell the scent and know which letter it was. For example, the students would smell the odors for the letters *h-e-l-l-o* and thus communicate through the sense of smell. Gallaudet thought this was wonderful, but it seems to have failed, mainly because Clerc couldn't use it; he had lost his sense of smell when he was two.

Gallaudet still wasn't satisfied with fingerspelling, so he decided to try another experiment. He invented the alphabet of facial expressions. It used facial expression for each letter. *A* was for awesome; *B* for boldness; *C* for curiosity; *D* for despair; *E* for eagerness; *F* for fear; *G* for gladness; and so forth. Can you imagine trying to spell through facial expressions and trying to understand what was being communicated? There are stories, though, about people using the alphabet of faces. Here is an example:

Many, many years ago, two deaf adults traveled together on a stagecoach from one town to another. They sat next to each other. Two hearing people sat across from them. The deaf passengers did not want to sign, so instead, they talked to each other with their facial expressions during the trip. The hearing people across from them kept trying to figure out what they were doing. (The reaction was similar to when you talk with your hands on a bus and the other passengers stare at you.)

Gallaudet and Clerc tried to find the best teaching methods while they worked together. After thirteen years at the school, Gallaudet decided to resign. Clerc chose to stay in America. He went back to visit his family and friends in France from time to time, but he ended up staying in the United States for forty-two years. Including his eight years of teaching in Paris, Clerc taught deaf children for fifty years. He devoted his full attention to helping deaf children. He never went to college; he had no time for himself. However, three colleges presented him with honorary degrees.

Clerc's mind came back to the present. There he was standing before all the people at the opening of Gallaudet College on June 28, 1864. He thought how wonderful it was to take part in the event. He began his speech and thanked the people for inviting him to see this most important day. It was a great honor for him. He spoke briefly. When he finished, the people applauded and the deaf people waved their handkerchiefs, again.

Laurent Clerc remained a Frenchman at heart even though he lived in America for many years. He was French, but people thought and spoke of him as an American. Deaf people call him "The Father of the American Instructors of the Deaf." When Clerc passed away in 1869, people contributed money to a memorial fund. Eventually, there was enough money to get a bust of Clerc made. The inscription on the bust says, "The Apostle of the Deaf Mutes of the New World." This line was taken from a letter written by Abbé Sicard to Clerc just before Clerc left for America. In his letter the Abbé said, "You are the apostle of the deaf mutes of the New World."

I must tell you that Clerc really is the greatest deaf teacher of all time!

CHAPTER 4

Me or We

Frank Turk

I want to talk to you young people about attitude. I have traveled to many schools for the deaf and have seen some students with good attitudes and some with bad attitudes. What is attitude? Some people think they know, but they really can't define it. I can tell you an easy trick on how to remember the meaning of attitude.

Attitude is divided into three areas: first, how you feel; second, how you act; and third, how you think. An adult many years ago impressed upon me that attitude is something you cannot take for granted. You can't get *fat* on attitude. The key word is fat. *F* is for how you feel; *A* is for how you act; and *T* is for how you think. F-A-T! If you take a quiz and your teacher asks you the meaning of attitude, you can answer it, "Attitude is how you feel, how you act, and how you think." You will probably get an *A* for that. Then I want you to write a letter of thanks to me for my help!

One thing I would like to change in young people is the *me* attitude. Young people who always ask, "What's in it for me?" have the *me* attitude. They don't understand the importance of having a *we* attitude. A *me* attitude is so-so, but a *we* is fine. Maybe you know someone with a *me* attitude, and you want to forget that person. No, you should keep that person in your life or in your group because he or she may have several important leadership traits. For example, that person may be an aggressive person. That's important. Many leaders, like Lyndon B. Johnson (LBJ) and John F. Kennedy (JFK), were successful because of their aggressive attitudes. Maybe you can help the aggressive person in your life or group. Work with him or her to change the *me* to a *we* attitude. Then the person will understand the importance of serving the group.

Another thing to emphasize is a positive attitude. For example, on TV you find weather reports on four or five channels. Your favorite may be Channel 5, another person's may be Channel 7, but my favorite is Channel 9. Why? The weather reporter on Channel 9 is very positive. He never uses the words *partly cloudy*. Instead he uses *partly sunny*. The words *partly cloudy* and *partly sunny* have the same meaning, but sunny is more pleasant, more positive. Partly cloudy sounds more negative.

Once, during my school days in Minnesota, I had a glass of water in my hand. An adult saw me with the glass in my hand and said, "If you were to write a sentence describing the glass of water you are holding, what would you say?"

I set the glass down and wrote, "The glass of water is half empty."

The adult looked at my sentence and said, "No, that is a negative sentence. You said the glass of water is half empty. Cross out the word *empty* and write the word *full*. That is a positive word."

I changed my sentence to say, "The glass of water is half full."

You must make every effort every day to be positive in your way of living, thinking, and feeling. When you do that, your English will be more positive. You can change the words around to make them more positive. This will help you develop the habit of being positive in whatever you do, even in difficult situations.

One sign I see many young people use which I don't like is the sign *can't. I can't, I can't, I can't*—I hate that sign. I hope all of you will throw the sign *can't* into your wastebasket. Throw it away and never pick it up again. Let your favorite sign be *can*. We deaf people can do anything if we are willing to try. Remember that.

An example of a person with a positive attitude is the famous man who invented the electric light bulb, Thomas Edison. How many times do you think he made mistakes before he succeeded in inventing the light bulb? I have asked many people around the country, and they have answered anywhere from a few to one thousand mistakes. Thomas Edison tried 17,143 times before he was successful in getting his light bulb to work. How many of you would be willing to make 17,143 mistakes before you succeeded once? I want you to remember when you make four or five mistakes in your English, you still have 17,139 more times to try before you succeed. But that is all right.

Mistakes can be wonderful teachers. Think of the pencil with an eraser on top. Why did the manufacturers make the pencil with an eraser? They make it because it is natural for people to make mistakes. It is all right, perfectly all right, to make mistakes. There is no shame in not knowing everything. Remember a pencil whenever you are in a situation and make a mistake.

Some years ago two famous deaf leaders, who didn't like each other, lived a block apart in a small town. Both of them were very successful in their areas of leadership, but they hated each other. When it came to leading and helping other people, though, they had a good "others before self" attitude. When the two of them were with a group, they understood that their personal feelings were secondary in importance. The cause they were helping with was of primary importance. They worked together, but they did not socialize at parties.

One afternoon the two men attended the same meeting. When they left the meeting and started home, it was raining hard. They lived near each other, and both decided to take the shortest and quickest way home. That way was via a railroad track, so they walked there through the mud. One man had on a new pair of shoes, and he was worried that his shoes would get dirty. He suggested to the other man that they walk on the tracks, one man on each rail. It was hard to balance on one rail, but they tried it. It didn't work, so one man said to the other, "Why don't you walk on one rail, and I will walk on the other rail. Then if we reach out and clasp hands, our balance problem will probably be eliminated." It was, and the two men arrived home without getting too muddy. They helped each other. That is an example of positive attitudes at work.

The last thing I would like to share with you in connection with attitude is that deaf youth around the country are afraid to ask questions. That is a mistake; it is almost a crime. When I was a little boy in the Minnesota School for the Deaf, I would not ask questions. Why? I was stubborn for one thing. Also, I didn't want people to think I was dumb. I really didn't want my rival in school to know that I didn't know something. My rival and I competed for the best grades, for more points in games, and for girl friends. I often felt like a blockhead in school. The teacher would write many words that I didn't understand on the chalkboard, but I would not raise my hand and ask the teacher to explain. I knew that my rival would think I was dumb. But he raised his hand; he had a positive attitude. He had the courage to ask questions: "What does that word mean?" he would ask the teacher.

The teacher would write more sentences on the board to explain the word and its meaning. I didn't know the word, but I would look at my rival and say, "You don't know that word? That is a baby word. I learned it two or three years ago."

That was really a lie. He would get mad and sit there thinking about beating me up later instead of listening to the teacher. I was very calm, listening to the teacher and trying to learn. That was selfish of me, and I don't want you to be like that.

Many years ago I had in my office a newspaper clipping from New York City. It was a true story and it was very interesting. One day a boy was walking along a busy street in New York. He stopped and looked up at a nearby building—the Empire State Building. He stood there and kept looking up at the building. Other people walking along saw him looking up. They stopped and started looking up, too. Soon the people began talking to each other about why they were looking up at the building. Different stories got started. One story was that someone up there wanted to jump, to commit suicide. Another story was that a bomb was in the building. The police came and got all of the people out of the Empire State Building. They cleared it because they thought there was some kind of danger. Before long, all of the surrounding streets were full of cars and people. The area was paralyzed. Nothing could move. Police checked the building with dogs, but they found no bomb. Then they began asking around among the people to find out what the problem was. They finally found the boy standing there looking up, the one who started it all. The police learned that he was blind; he wasn't looking at anything, really. If the first person who saw the boy looking up had gone to the trouble of asking him what was wrong up there, all of these problems could have been avoided. Just asking a question was all that was needed.

Many words go by without your understanding them. Don't let that happen. Stop and ask someone what they mean. When they are explained, put them in your mental file cabinet. Don't be afraid to ask questions. Become the person you are meant to be.

Look or Listen

Ray S. Parks, Jr.

A long time ago, when I was sixteen, I got my driver's license. I wanted to drive, so I asked my dad if I could use his car. He thought about it and said, "Well, it will be okay, but only for short distances." I started driving his car for short distances. By the time I was seventeen years old, Dad saw that my driving was good, so he let me drive more. I felt so good in my dad's big Buick—at that time it was a great car—driving around waving at everybody. I enjoyed having people look at me.

One day I decided to drive up to the mountains. I saw a man hitchhiking. I pulled over and he got in the car. He spoke to me, but I motioned to him that I couldn't hear. He looked at me and pointed for me to drive straight ahead. I nodded and drove on. As I was going up the road, I decided to pass a car. My passenger became nervous; he just couldn't sit still. He kept bothering me and saying, "You can't drive; you can't hear. How can you drive when you can't hear?" He kept saying the same things over and over.

Then I got an idea. I remembered that I had some tape in the glove compartment of the car. I pulled off to the side of the road. The man looked at me like he wanted to know what as going on. I motioned to him that he should drive. He thought that was a great idea. "Just a minute," I said. "You need to hear to drive, right?"

He said, "Yes, that's right."

So I tore off a piece of the tape, a big piece of tape, and put it over the man's eyes. Of course, he couldn't see. I said, "Okay, go ahead and drive."

"I can't drive," he said. "I can't see!"

He learned that you can drive without hearing but not without seeing.

The Case of the Missing Scissors

Barbara Kannapell

My father told me many stories. He was deaf and loved to tell stories in sign language. One story he told was about his father, my grandfather. One day my grandfather had to go to the hospital because he had trouble with his appendix. He had an operation and, a few days later, went home in a horse and buggy. When he arrived home, he still had pain in his side. The pain lasted for days, so grandfather had to go back to the hospital. The doctor said he would have to open the incision. When the doctor reopened the incision, he found a small pair of scissors inside my grandfather. After my grandfather learned this, he became furious and wanted to sue the hospital. His doctor was worried. He didn't want to be sued, so he said to my grandfather, "Okay, the operation and everything is free!"

That Look of Envy

Jack R. Gannon

My deaf friend Tom told me this story. I would like to share it with you. Tom had a beautiful car, a roadster (a sports car) called an MG. Tom was very proud of his car. It was a beautiful shade of red and it had shiny chrome.

One day after work, Tom was driving along on his way home. He stopped at a red light, and he noticed people glancing at him. He felt proud. The people were noticing his little red car. Feeling good, he shifted gears and revved up his car and drove on. Soon he arrived at another stop light. He noticed more people staring, more than before, and he felt inspired. He looked at his watch and drove on. When he arrived home, he drove into his driveway. His neighbor came running out, waving at him, and shouting, "Hey, Tom! Hey, Tom! Your horn is stuck!"

A Little Bit at a Time

Mary Beth Miller

I remember when I was a small girl, I loved to eat peanut butter. One day I told my mother I wanted a peanut butter sandwich. She said, "No, it is too close to dinner."

"Please," I said, but she replied, "No."

Again I said, "Please, I want a peanut butter sandwich."

My mother said no, again, and she looked angry.

I said, "Okay," and started to go outside. My mother had a visitor in another room, so she went in there.

As I was going out, I stopped, changed my mind, and went back into the kitchen. I opened the cupboard, took out a gigantic jar of peanut butter, unscrewed the lid, and took out a huge lump of peanut butter. Then I put the jar back. As I started out again, I saw my mother coming in. I was frightened because she had said that I couldn't have a peanut butter sandwich, but I had gotten some peanut butter to eat, anyway. I quickly put the whole lump in my mouth. I swallowed, but the peanut butter got stuck. I started to choke on it; I couldn't breathe! I walked along the side of my house holding my throat. I felt faint and couldn't hold my head up.

The friend who was talking with my mother looked out the window and noticed that something was wrong with me. She said to my mother, "You had better check on your daughter; something may be wrong."

Mother opened the door and saw me there with my mouth open. She was scared. She thought something was stuck in my throat, but she didn't know what it was. She ran down the steps, took my legs, turned me upside down, and shook me up and down. People passing by stopped their cars and stared. They wondered what my mother was doing, shaking me up and down. Finally the lump of peanut butter came out. Then Mother turned me over and stood me up. She was surprised when she looked down and saw the lump of peanut butter. She thought maybe it had been a button or a coin that I choked on, but it wasn't. It was that peanut butter. Oh, my throat hurt! All my mother said was, "Well." But I learned my lesson. From that time on I've never taken a huge lump of peanut butter—only a little bit at a time.

CHAPTER 5

The Importance of Bilingual Education for Deaf People

Barbara Kannapell

A few years ago I became interested in studying different sign languages and deaf people's use of different signs. Since I was studying sign languages, I decided to go to school and take some courses in sociolinguistics. I was fascinated to learn that foreign people's use of French and Spanish parallel deaf people's use of different sign languages. It was very interesting. Sociolinguistics itself tends to look at things in more positive ways.

More recently I investigated different professional textbooks about deaf children. I didn't realize that deaf people, including deaf children, are given so many negative labels. For example, some of the labels are language deficient; learning disabled, meaning one can't learn or has problems in learning; and possessing a communication disorder. Do we have a communication disorder? No, we do not. We deaf adults and children do fine in sign language, but hearing people who evaluate us label us as language deficient. That is an error. I think the labels have influenced deaf children in how they feel about themselves. I think the labels have influenced how I feel about myself. I became negative, I had a negative self-image. I thought hearing people were better than I because they had fantastic English and good speech. Negative labels made me think this way.

Today, many people use total communication. Is that more positive? I think it is more positive to use different ways to communicate with deaf children. I notice many schools like the idea of using the term total communication. I notice many teachers speaking and signing at the same time, but that is all. I think total communication means using other methods, including American Sign Language (ASL). ASL is used by deaf people throughout the United States.

If you include ASL, then I think that is the true meaning of total communication.

I want to suggest looking for more positive labels for deaf children. I also propose the idea of bilingual education for deaf children. They already know ASL, so why not help them make the connection between ASL and English. Really, deaf children know many things in ASL, but they don't know what those things mean in English. If the teacher knows English, but not ASL, and the deaf children know ASL, but not English, they can work together, exchange information, and help each other. For example, deaf children might say in ASL, "McDonald's is my favorite restaurant. It has delicious hamburgers." They can say this in signs, but they don't know how to write the English sentences. If the teacher knows ASL, she or he can explain how to write the words in English. That is why I like the idea of bilingual education for deaf children. If deaf children know both ASL and English, they can be called bilingual. Children who only know ASL can be called ASL monolingual, monolingual meaning one language. Deaf children who know only English can be called English monolingual. Deaf children need such positive labels to improve their self-image.

Life with Brian

Eric Malzkuhn

I am going to share some very wonderful moments of my life with you. I have three boys; no, really, I have four. The first three are my sons, and the fourth is my dog. My second son is deaf. (My dog is hearing, by the way.) I want to tell you about some incidents in the life of my deaf son which show the growth of his imagination and language, and his growth in other ways.

One early incident I remember happened one night while I was sitting very comfortably reading the newspaper. Brian, who was about three years old, ran up to me. He didn't have much language at that time. "Daddy, Daddy," he said.

"Yes, what is it?" I asked.

"Daddy, Daddy," he said again. Then he made a gesture which I had never seen before. It was very strange. I didn't know how to respond, so I got up and followed him. He ran quickly to the door; we opened it, and sure enough, I had forgotten something. It was Halloween. There stood a boy with a sheet on his head and a grimace on his face. Brian's gesture had very clearly communicated what it was. It was his own invention, and it was probably better than the sign "ghost."

As Brian grew a little older, he became interested in many things. Mostly he was interested in trains. He had many different kinds of trains, which I had given him, but I wanted to give him something related to his trains for Christmas. I tried to ask him what he wanted, but he didn't have the words to explain. I asked him what it looked like. He showed me, and it was obvious he wanted a semaphore for his trains. That was what I gave him for Christmas.

Our communication progressed. One day I had to go to the doctor. The whole family went with me. When we got to the office, we went in and sat down. Soon Brian became restless. He wanted to go over to the corner and play with the toys. I told him it was okay. A while later an old woman walked in and sat down in the chair Brian had used. Brian was busy playing; then he suddenly looked up and became very upset. He didn't like it that the woman was in his chair. Brian came over to the woman and said, "Hey." He tapped her on the leg and signed to her, "That's mine. That's mine. That's my chair." I didn't know what to do. I was so embarrassed; people were looking at me. I told Brian to be quiet. "That's wrong, it's mine; it's my chair," Brian said. The woman was quite uncomfortable so she got up and left. Later, I told Brian to be kind to ladies. That was one of his first lessons in life!

On one of my bowling nights I was backing out of the driveway when I saw Brian on his bicycle. He stopped, stood up on the seat, reached up, and pulled the fire alarm near our house. I stopped, ran inside, and told my wife that Brian had pulled the fire alarm. My wife said, "Really? That is your responsibility; you saw him." She was right, but I took off to bowl. My wife told me later what happened. Fire engines came racing up our street and stopped in front of our house. Brian was shocked, but fascinated. The fire chief strutted right up to our house and looked around. My wife wrote a note to the fire chief which said, "He did it." She pointed to Brian. My Brian was all starry-eyed. The fire chief looked down at him and asked, "You did it?" Then he began to speak rapidly.

My wife said, "Brian can't hear."

So the fire chief began to gesture. He said, "No, no, no. That is bad."

From then on when Brian went past a fire alarm, he said, "No, red box, no." Blue, red, and white box—a mailbox—it was okay to pull down the handle, but not on a red fire alarm—no!

As Brian grew older, he began to understand more and more. His interests also began to change. One time he came home looking angry. "What's wrong? Why are you angry?" I asked him.

"I went to the boy's club," he said, "and the director told me to go home."

"What were you doing? Why were you sent home?" I wanted to know.

He answered, "I was playing."

"Playing," I said. "Brian, what were you playing?"

"I was playing the piano," he replied. I found out later why the director sent Brian home. (Remember, Brian is deaf, and he was playing the piano!) The director had gone to Brian and asked him what he was doing. Brian had responded, "I am playing the piano."

"No, you are not," the director said. "Go home."

Apparently Brian had hit the wrong chord or something.

This next incident demonstrates how Brian showed some interest in responsibility. He wanted to do things to help at home because he wanted an allowance. He asked me if he could do some work. I said he could and asked what he wanted to do. He didn't know. I suggested that he take his brother Max for a walk around the block. I told him I would pay him. That was fine with Brian, so he took his little brother, and they walked down the street. I watched them leave, and then I started working. A little while later Brian came back alone.

My wife looked at him and said, "Brian, where is Max?"

Brian said, "Poor Max, he was on the railroad tracks, and the train ran over him and he was cut in half. There was a lot of blood."

My wife got in the car and hurried to the train depot. She saw nothing; no one was there. Brian was sitting in the back seat of the car. "Where is Max," she asked again.

"Oh, he is in the cemetery," Brian answered.

My wife drove to the cemetery and there was Max, crying and crying.

Later my wife asked Brian, "Why did you tell that awful story?"

"Well," he said, "I wanted to make an interesting story. It was very interesting!"

To show you that growth does not stop and older deaf people have problems occasionally, let me share a final experience I had with Brian. One day, while Brian was still living at home, my wife was obviously not feeling her best. How did I know? She began to slam the cupboard doors. (That is always my signal to sit down quietly and hide behind the newspaper. I peek out occasionally to see what is happening.) That day while I was hiding behind the newspaper, Brian walked into the house dribbling a basketball—pound, pound, pound—and went to his room.

In a little while I could see the walls vibrating. I went in Brian's room and found a big argument going on between him and his brother Max. "All right, settle down," I said. (I am a father so I have to play referee once in awhile.) I said to the boys, "What is the matter?" I heard one explanation and then the other explanation. Brian said Max was wrong, and Max said Brian was wrong.

It seems that Max had said to Brian, "Mother has a headache, and you are not helping any."

Brian had said, "I helped her all morning. I helped her clean the house."

You see, he misunderstood the idiom, "not helping any." To Brian it meant that he had not helped clean the house. To Max it meant that Brian's basketball dribbling bothered their mother: it was making things worse.

Brian is grown now, and he is a man in every sense of the word. He is a teacher of the deaf; maybe he faces the same problems that I faced. Although I think that Brian gave us a lot of problems and a lot of worries, if I had my way, I would have three more sons just like him!

CHAPTER 6

Applause for Eyes to See

Bernard Bragg

I remember how excited I was when I sat down in front of the mirror, opened a jar of white clown make-up, and began to smear it on my face. Looking back, I remembered when I was a little boy, watching my father perform on stage, acting in sign language. I was both thrilled and motivated. I guess that was how I became interested in theater. Much later I met Marcel Marceau, the world-famous mime, and he invited me to Paris to study with him.

But there I was, sitting in front of the mirror in a dressing room of a nightclub. I picked up the black pencil and used it around my face, under my eyes, and around my lips. I put some red make-up on my lips. Then I began to feel a little nervous and scared because tonight I was going to do my first performance in that big place. A lot of people were coming to see me perform. Would I succeed, or would I fail?

Suddenly the door opened and the manager—Frey was his name—stuck his head through the door. "You're on," he said.

"Okay," I replied. I put on a red and white striped shirt and white pants and ran out on the dark stage. I stood and waited for the lights to go on. When they did, I saw many people sitting and looking at me. I performed several different sketches. People began to enjoy them, and they started to applaud after each one. I acted out different characters: An old lady hobbling along with a cane, a big pot-bellied man with a mustache and beard listening to his stopwatch, and a little boy hopping along with a dog on a leash. Finally I was done. I bowed and all the people clapped and cheered. Saying good-bye, I left the stage. After I left, the manager went on stage and stopped the applause. "It is no use to applaud," he told the people. "The man you just saw is deaf. So why applaud? Don't bother!"

I was in my dressing room. Someone came in and asked, "Do you know what Frey said?"

"No," I said, "what?"

"He said it is useless to applaud because you are deaf."

I was shocked. Because I'm deaf he was telling people not to applaud. I ran back on the stage. "Hold it, hold it," I told the audience. "I can't hear, it's true, but I have eyes and I can see your hands clapping. So come on, applaud." And sure enough, all the people applauded. I said good-bye and left the stage again.

On My Own

Deborah M. Sonnenstrahl

When I was a little girl, about five years old, I went to an oral school in Baltimore, Maryland. At that time I was living in a house with my family which consisted of my mother and father, my grandmother and grandfather, and a great-aunt. Everyone was hearing except me. I was born deaf. Naturally, they made every effort to include me in all activities. They loved me, but sometimes I thought perhaps they loved me too much; I was overprotected. The result of that was that I often wanted to show my independence. I became rebellious from time to time. I wanted to show them I knew how to act like a grown-up. I was no exception; I was just like any other child.

One bright Saturday morning I made a formal announcement to my family. I said, "I am going out for a walk. I have decided where I will go."

My family said, "Oh, really! That's fine. Where are you going?"

"I am going to visit my school," I said.

The oral school was about five blocks away from our house. Every morning the school bus came by, picked me up, and took me to school, but that special Saturday morning I wanted to walk to school. It didn't matter that the school was closed for the day. That was not important to me. My grandmother opened the closet door and got her coat. She was ready to go with me. I asked here, "Where are you going?"

She answered, "I'm going with you."

"No," I said, "you are not going with me; I am going alone."

"Alone? No, no, no! You can't go alone."

"Why not?"

"But, Debbie, you live five blocks from school. You will have to cross busy streets. Cars will come, and they might hit you. You can't go alone; you can't hear the cars."

I had already made up my mind. "I am going alone!" I screamed.

Then my family started to argue among themselves. My mother and grandmother were saying, "No, no, she can't go, she can't go, she can't go." I started to cry. In the middle of all that my father stood up, thoughtfully surveyed the situation, and made up his mind. He said, "Let her go." He tapped me on the shoulder and said, "You can go alone."

"Oh, Daddy, Daddy!" I cried, jumping for joy. I put on my coat, scarf, and gloves. I was so excited! For the first time ever, I was going out in the world by myself. My mother cried. She looked at me; my grandmother looked at me; my great-aunt looked at me. My grandfather just stood by the door with his cane, acting very cool about the situation. My father, who was a pediatrician (a baby doctor), walked into his office. I waved good-bye to each member of the family. I kissed each one on the cheek and went out all by myself. I was alone, breathing in the free air.

It was a strange feeling. I was walking to school alone! On my way I began to notice things I had never seen before. I had passed this way many, many times with my mother, my grandmother, or my aunt. It didn't matter because they were always holding my hand and I was looking down. I never really looked at the world around me. But this time on my own, I started to look at things. I noticed my dentist's house. It had venetian blinds, and I had never seen them before. Oh, and a store had a special name printed on it! Another house had fancy flowers in front of it. I looked around and enjoyed my walk very much. I arrived at the first intersection and stood there. Oh, I felt so grown up; I felt so adult. I looked around for cars. When the coast was clear, I jumped across the street. I ran. I was safe. I was free! I felt so good.

I was walking the second block when I began to feel that something was strange, something was out of the ordinary. I looked around, thinking perhaps people were watching me. No, that wasn't it; people were passing by, and they were minding their own business. I looked up. There was nothing there. I felt strange, but I tried to ignore the feeling and continued walking.

In the third block the same thing happened. I felt strange again, so I hurried along. I reached the fourth block, and then I saw my school. Oh, this was my old friend where I spent five days a week. There it was, but I had the strange feeling again. Something was bothering me, but I saw nothing. Then I looked behind me. Do you know what? My father was following me! Oh, I felt defeated!

The Stand-in

Eric Malzkuhn

I am going to tell you about a precious moment in my life—something that will never happen to me again. While I was living in California, I taught several different kinds of classes. Two of the classes were drama classes. One was a class of slow learning students. For this class I picked a play called *Amahl and the Night Visitors,* based on an opera by Gian Carlo Menotti. You have probably seen the play on television. The play was a good choice for the students in that particular class because the lines were not very long. The students struggled with the short lines. They memorized them. Then, they practiced and practiced and practiced. They worked hard for me. When opening night came and the curtain opened, I stood and watched. I just couldn't believe it. It was beautiful. The play was fantastic. The students did a fine job. I was so proud of the class because the play was a real success.

When the curtain closed, Johnny, who acted the part of Amahl, came up to me and said, "Hey, tomorrow I can't act in the play."

"What? You can't act?" I asked. "What are you talking about? What do you mean? People are coming tomorrow to see the play. You have to be here."

"Well," Johnny replied, "my father says I have to go to the dentist to have a tooth pulled."

Oh, no, I was stuck. What was I going to do? I thought and in a little while, I had an idea. Amahl was a crippled boy. Well, I am crippled, too; Amahl's leg was crippled like mine. Maybe I could change Amahl from the son to the father. I considered this and decided the change would be okay.

That night I went home and studied my lines. I studied them all night—all night, I tell you. But I wasn't alone. My three dogs helped me. Oh, they were wonderful. We paced back and forth, back and forth, all four of us. If I dropped a line, the dogs sat. If I messed up a line, the dogs barked. And if I just happened to be on the wrong page, my dogs growled. That way it was hard for me to make a mistake. I just followed what they told me what to do while I practiced all night. The next day I drove to school. I felt tired, my eyes were blurry, and my mind was fuzzy, but I was excited. I was ready for the performance.

During the play I made one mistake, just one. The girl who played the role of the mother, you remember, was supposed to be a slow learner. I had changed the lead role from the son to the father. She had to call Amahl father instead of son all through the play. She didn't make a single mistake! Now who was slow and who was smart?

Our Paths Crossed Again

Thomas A. Mayes

Imagine that each of us, at one time in our lives, has had some experience, some encounter, which demonstrates that this world, even though it is 25,000 miles in circumference with over 200 billion people, is really very small. I would like to share such an experience with you.

Back in 1960 I was a doctoral student at Michigan State University in East Lansing. One of the courses I took was a seminar called "Personnel Management in Higher Education." The group was small, about twelve people, but we had many interesting discussions. We decided that for the last meeting of the class, we would invite the three highest administrators of the university—the president, the provost, and of course, the football coach—to join us for dinner. We would talk with them and pick their brains.

It so happened that the man who sat next to me was the provost; his name was Paul A. Miller. Paul Miller, a very intelligent man, had a position of high authority in a university of forty to forty-five thousand students. I did not feel very comfortable sitting next to him, and I do not think he felt very comfortable sitting next to me. He had never seen nor met a deaf person before in his life, and I had never met a provost before. He had a feeling that if he talked to me, I would not understand him. And I felt, also, that if I talked to him, he wouldn't understand me. So Dr. Miller and I spent a very quiet evening together.

About a year later Paul Miller left MSU to become president of West Virginia University. He stayed there one or two years; then he became Assistant Secretary of the Department of Health, Education, and Welfare and moved to Washington, D.C. In that capacity, Dr. Miller served as a liaison to Gallaudet College, and he attended all of the Board of Trustee meetings on Kendall Green. He developed a very great interest in deaf people and in Gallaudet College. His relationship with Gallaudet became stronger. About three years or so later, he moved to one of the southern states to teach, and then he went to the Rochester Institute of Technology in New York. There he was the president of the mother institution of the National Technical Institute for the Deaf.

Gallaudet College had faith in Paul Miller and wanted to continue its relationship with him. So the college invited Dr. Miller to serve on the Board of Trustees as a regular member.

Some years passed, and in 1968 I was invited to serve on the Board of Trustees. When I came to my first board meeting, I found myself sitting next to Paul A. Miller.

Caught in a Riot

Michael Schwartz

Once I was in Mexico with a group of high school students. We stopped in a town called Oaxaca. (It's a funny name, and I really don't know how to pronounce it.) We arrived there in a Volkswagen bus, maybe fifteen of us in all. When we got to Oaxaca, we spread out and went to different places. I was with one of my friends, and we decided to have something to drink. We went into a restaurant and ordered drinks. All of a sudden my friend heard some noise outside. He told me that he heard something, but he didn't know what it was. Then we saw some people running very quickly past the restaurant. Of course, we became curious. We wondered what they were doing, and where they were going. We decided to follow them.

We quickly paid the bill, went outside, and ran to catch up with the people. We began following them. When they turned a corner, so did we. We came to a stop across the street from a large building. People were throwing stones through the windows of the building. We learned that students inside the building had taken control of it. They had taken control of the building to publicize their demands. My friend and I—we were curious to find out more about what was going on—stayed there. That wasn't a smart thing to do because a few minutes later a big truck pulled up outside the building. A lot of men jumped out of the truck. It turned out that they were soldiers. Naturally, we were frightened, but we still stayed. We wanted to see what was going to happen. The students retreated inside the building and refused to come out. The soldiers became very angry and started shooting. My friend and I didn't know what to do, whether to stay or run. People were running about, and we had to make a decision. There was no more time to think.

We ran! We came to a church and went inside. Many other people were in the church because they thought they would be safe there.

They knew that the soldiers wouldn't go in the church. While we waited, we remembered that we had come with a group, but now there was just the two of us. Where was the rest of the group? We didn't know. We were pretty scared because the soldiers were shooting and the people were throwing rocks. We stayed in the church and talked about what to do. Finally, we decided to leave and try to find the restaurant again. Maybe some people in our group would be there.

I thought I remembered the way, so we left the church and ran. I was right; we found the restaurant. Some of the people from our group were there. We all got together and ran back to the bus. By that time, the town was in an uproar. There was lots of noise—people running and shouting, soldiers shooting—it was really terrible. When we got in our VW bus, we took off like a shot. As we drove through the town, we saw some women carrying sticks. They were big, mean looking women. They were walking in the direction of the building where the students were. We didn't know why. Later we found out that the women were the mothers of the students, and they were angry with the soldiers for shooting at their children.

As I look back on that experience, I was afraid, nervous, and excited while it was happening. Now I'd like to have more experiences like that.

My ABC Book

Mary Beth Miller

For a long time I wanted to write a book, a sign language book. I thought about it, and finally I wrote an ABC book. Oh, it wasn't very good, but the drawings in it were fine. My problem was how to get it published.

One day I flew to Paris, France, and met my friend Remy. I told him that I wanted to publish my ABC book. He asked to see it, so I showed him the book. He thumbed through it and then put it down. He said he too wanted to publish a book, an ABC book. He asked if we could work together on one. I agreed. I was so excited when I returned to the United States.

Several months passed, and then Remy and I met again. We had to make plans for our book. What words and pictures would we use for the letters of the alphabet? What would stand for the letter A? Angel. What would we use for the letter B? Bug, butterfly. We had to make decisions about words and signs for all the letters. Then I called some friends and asked them if they wanted to have their pictures taken for the book Remy and I were writing. They accepted gladly, so we had many pictures taken.

The photographer, George, couldn't sign; he didn't know signs at all. If I talked to him, he didn't understand, so we struggled, writing notes back and forth. Remy knew signs a bit. He wasn't skilled in signing, but he tried hard to communicate. The three of us managed to work well together on the book. When George finished taking all the pictures, we met to choose the ones to use. We looked through thousands of pictures, throwing out the lousy ones and keeping the good ones. While we worked, my two friends improved their signing. George, who couldn't sign at first, learned thank you, happy, play, picture, now, again, and many other signs. Remy, who could sign some, improved and became a very good signer.

When the book was published and I received a copy, I was very proud. I felt good. Seeing it gave me goose pimples. I was extremely happy. Remy and George were happy, too. Our book was finished, and it was beautiful. I was happy because many of my friends' pictures were in the book. Now every day I can look at our book and think about my many wonderful friends

CHAPTER 7

Deaf Pilots

Jack R. Gannon

I have learned, to my surprise, that through the years many deaf people have been licensed to fly planes. Almost one hundred deaf people have probably received a license at one time or another.

Nellie Willhite of South Dakota was the first woman and the first deaf person in the United States to get a pilot's license. She was a very successful pilot. She barnstormed around the Midwest, going to county fairs and doing stunt flying for crowds of impressed people. When she landed, she offered rides to the people, charging fifty cents for children and a dollar for adults. The first deaf man in this country to get his license to fly was John Stirling. This was in 1937. Ten years later, Rhulin Thomas, another deaf man, flew a small Piper Cub from Delaware to the west coast, becoming the first deaf person to fly solo across the United States.

I called the FAA, the Federal Aviation Agency, and inquired as to how many licensed pilots today are deaf. I was told that about twenty-five pilots are deaf. One of these is a commercial pilot. How about that?

Experience Is a Great Teacher

Florence B. Crammatte

E xperience is a great teacher. It teaches us many things: happiness and sadness; excitement and tranquility; success and failure; and from all these we learn wisdom. We learn a lot of information from books, but what we learn from experience makes a deeper impression on us and stays in our minds much longer.

In our lives we have many experiences that are ordinary and pass from our minds quickly. Other experiences have a profound impact on our lives. I have two experiences from my youth I would like to share with you.

While I was in school at the Alabama Institute for the Deaf, there was a very fat little girl there who was about ten years old. Her name was Annie, and she had a strange body odor. No matter what was done—washing two or three times a day, or changing her clothes every day—she still had this strange odor. Children can be cruel to each other; they criticized and insulted Annie constantly. The other children held their noses or ran the other way when they saw Annie coming. I was guilty of doing that. When I went home for the summer, I described Annie to my mother with much disgust. My mother looked sad and said, "Poor child." That was all she said. I was somewhat nonplussed. Through the summer I often remembered what my mother had said, and my attitude became more understanding. I began to understand how Annie must have felt, and I resolved to be nice to her.

That fall Annie did not come back to school, and I never saw or heard of her again. That lesson has stayed with me through all these years. I have tried to be understanding of people who have faults or problems they cannot help. I try to help people who are shy, or who have bad tempers, or have a hard time explaining their ideas; newcomers who feel uncomfortable; or people who might lack self-confidence.

The other experience, one which I cherish, happened during my first year at Gallaudet College. I was seventeen years old then. We had a very active chapter in the YWCA (Young Women's Christian Association). The most enthusiastic supporter was Dr. Elizabeth Peet, the Dean of Women. For our Christmas project we decided to buy twelve dolls, sew clothes for them, and give them to poor children. One night the chapter president brought in twelve dolls and gave them out. Dr. Peet was with us that night, and she suggested that we give a tea when we had finished dressing the dolls. We would invite the students and faculty to see our efforts. Dr. Peet will give prizes for the prettiest doll, the neatest doll, and the most colorful doll. My friend Isobol[3] and I worked together on a doll. Another girl, Ruth, quickly went to her closet, pulled out one of her most beautiful

---

[3] *My friend Isobol later married an Episcopal minister. He was a minister to the deaf in northern New York State.*

evening gowns, and began to rip it up to make a dress for her doll. When Isobol and I saw that, we decided we couldn't compete with her for the most beautiful doll, so we decided to try for the neatest doll.

We worked hard on our doll and her clothes. We sewed with care and patience. On the day of the tea we placed our doll among the other dolls. They had been placed on a long table in the girls' reading room. What a lovely sight they were! There was Ruth's doll in a beautiful blue taffeta dress with ruffles down the skirt, and little pink flowers all over. Our doll was dressed in a white blouse, plaid skirt, and plaid beret. Dr. Peet was one of the judges and she announced the winners. Ruth's doll won the prize for the having the prettiest dress. Dr. Peet said the judges had trouble deciding which was the neatest doll. They felt that our doll should win, but there was something not quite right about it. She picked up our doll and pointed to some threads, little threads hanging from one sleeve and from the skirt. She said they should have been cut off. How crestfallen we were! The prizes were one dollar each. That was in the days of the Great Depression, and one dollar was a good amount of money.

Isobol and I learned our lesson, and I have never forgotten it. Every time I sew, I think about Dr. Peet and that doll. When I finish sewing something, I look it over inside and out to make sure no threads are hanging.

I cherish that small memory of Dr. Peet and me. I have told the story many times. I told it to my two daughters when they started sewing. Both of them had a good laugh, but I know that they remember the story and they have learned from it, too.

U.S.S. *Thomas Hopkins Gallaudet*

Jack R. Gannon

Did you know that during World War II there was a ship named after Thomas Hopkins Gallaudet? The ship was christened with a bottle of champagne by Pearl S. Buck, the famous author. I don't remember the exact words she used, but she said something like this, "This ship was built by strong hands and named after a wonderful soul. Let this ship sail across the rough seas just like Gallaudet himself did."

After the ship was christened, it was loaned to Russia under the United States' lend-lease program. Russia used it during World War II. When the war was over, the Russians gave the ship back to America. For several years it was sold and resold; it was used by different countries for a variety of things.

Sometime in 1969, the ship was sailing from Guam to South Korea with a full load of scrap iron. It was hit by a bad storm and broke into two pieces. It sank off the coast of Japan. It was really sad, but the ship had served all over the world for thirty-five years.

Here We Go Again

Nancy Rarus

I am from a deaf family. My parents, my grandmother and grandfather, and my brother are all deaf. When I was growing up, I signed all the time. Oh, my mother and father required me to talk, too. My father always spoke to me in straight English. My mother did too. I went to a public school (P.S. 47) all through my childhood. The teachers there slapped my hands and wouldn't allow me to sign. At home I could sign, so I was safe.

When we sat around the dinner table at home, my mother would always say to my father, "Stop talking and let the children eat before the food gets cold." My father would answer, "No, the food is still hot." Then they would argue about that. The point is that when we were growing up, my mother and father always shared information, world news, and gossip with us. I enjoyed that.

I remember when I was at school, I would bring home a girl friend. The best part of her visit was the communication at the dinner table, the family discussions. We sat at the table a long time. My mother, who is a perfect housekeeper, liked to clean up as soon as possible. Most evenings she had to sit and wait for us to finish our discussions.

When I was in college and brought home a friend, we went through the same thing. One friend of mine had a huge family, she had many brothers and sisters. Her family always just sat and ate. Then they excused themselves and left the table. At my home it was different. This is one good memory I have of growing up in a deaf family.

I often went to visit deaf girl friends at their homes. Their parents were hearing. They couldn't communicate, so they wrote notes. I thought, "Hearing parents are writing notes with their children?" Oh, I felt bad for them. I realized how lucky I was.

My father was a very good speech teacher. He taught me many ways to pronounce different words; he even taught me some French words. He would correct me when I made mistakes. Now I don't have problems with the words he taught me, even the big words. I may have problems with small easy words—sometimes I can't say them to save my life—but big words like *gesundheit* I am skilled at; I can say those!

I remember something else from when I was small. I got so tired of my parents' friends who came to visit and said, "Oh, I remember when you were small; you were so cute. Now you are big. You have really grown." I would say, "Yeah." Sometimes they would say, "I doubt if you remember me. You were small . . ."

It was the same old thing. I said to myself, "In the future, when I grow up, I will not say those things to children." But I have to admit that I have been doing exactly the same thing. I guess it is part of human nature that we say those things.

Another thing that bothers me is how fast rumors spread among deaf children. Children of hearing parents are really lucky. Often the parents know nothing of what is happening with their deaf children. If I did something I didn't want my parents to know, I did it and that was it. However, soon there would be a tap on my shoulder. My parents knew; the rumors had spread like wildfire. I sympathize with deaf children with deaf parents because I know what they're going through.

Now, the tables are turned. I have two deaf children. I remember when my first child was born, the doctor informed me that he was deaf. I looked at the doctor and said "He's deaf! Ah, here we go again."

The Letter I Wrote, but Never Mailed

Barbara Kannapell

I was born deaf to deaf parents. It seems that it would have been easy for them to make a decision about which school was best for me, but that was not true. I think it was difficult because of the pressure of hearing relatives. For example, my grandmother worried about me. She wanted me to have good training in speech and lipreading. My parents sent me to a public school which had a special class for deaf children. I was four, and I remember that time very clearly. I went into the school and I tried to learn to talk and lipread, but when I went home, I signed to my parents.

One day a well-known person, Mrs. Spencer Tracy, came to visit the school. (She is famous for promoting the oral method and for teaching parents how to communicate with young deaf children.) Mrs. Tracy stood next to my grandmother, both of them watched me. Mrs. Tracy looked down at me—she looked so tall to me—and said, "How are you?"

I replied, "I am fine." I spoke; I didn't sign.

She said, "Oh, that is wonderful; that is marvelous."

That's all I can remember that happened to me in the oral school where I remained for six years. Then I transferred to a school for the deaf. I don't know why or how, but all of a sudden I transferred to the Kentucky School for the Deaf.

I entered my first class in that school in the middle of the school year. My mother and I went into the classroom, and the woman who would be my teacher came up to me. She said, "Take your coat off."

I didn't understand her so I looked at my mother for help. My mother remained quiet, so I looked back and the teacher said, "Take your coat off."

I still didn't understand her so I looked at my mother again. She was still quiet; I looked back at the teacher. I struggled for several minutes. Finally I understood—she wanted me to take my coat off. I took it off and hung it up.

That school emphasized oralism even though the teachers used signs. The good thing about the school was that I could use signs with deaf children outside and then use the oral method in the classroom. When I transferred to a third school, it was even better because the teachers used signs, and the children used signs. Only the supervisors did not use signs; they couldn't sign! Can you imagine that the supervisors, who took care of the children every night after school, looked after them, and supervised them, didn't know how to sign? When I did something wrong, the supervisor would slap my hands, but she couldn't sign at all. Sometimes I wanted to tell her what was wrong—that she should let me explain and that she shouldn't slap my hand—but the supervisor would say no and shake her head. That was it. I never thought of a supervisor as my friend.

Recently I found my old suitcase and opened it. Instantly I spotted a letter. "What's that?" I thought. I didn't remember writing a letter. The envelope was addressed to the superintendent of the school I attended. I was curious as to what I had said in the letter. I opened it and was surprised to read the things I wrote. It said something like this: If I had my way, I would make all supervisors learn sign language. It's too bad I never sent the letter to the superintendent of the school. Today, I notice many teachers learning signs and more supervisors learning them, too. I think that is marvelous!

My Present Aspiration

Ray S. Parks, Jr.

I would like to tell you how it feels growing up as a deaf person, and how I feel as a deaf person today. I can remember where I went to school when I was five years old, and what it was like growing up in a school for the deaf. I would go away to school in the fall and come home in the summer. I attended that school from the time I was five until I graduated from high school. I loved the school; many things were good in that school, but still, there were a few things that I didn't like that could have been changed.

I attended Gallaudet College and I enjoyed my years there. I became a teacher, and after college I taught in several different schools for the deaf. I found a lot of things in these schools that I really didn't like, things that I thought could be better. However, the administration acted like it was frozen; it was like the administrators were afraid to change things. They felt that if they changed, everything would be chaotic. Things had to be kept under control, and all the children had to fit into one mold.

I saw this happening, and I didn't like it. I wanted the children to develop independent thinking, to think freely, but it never happened. As a result I decided to get out of the educational world and join the National Theatre of the Deaf (NTD). During my two years with them as an actor, I thought I was out of the educational world and in the world of the theater. I was wrong; while I was with NTD, I became more and more immersed in the educational world. I traveled to schools, gave workshops, and developed plays and similar things for the schools. I found that I was even more sensitive to the situations in the schools, the things I had seen as a teacher.

After two years with NTD I decided to go to New York University and study for a Ph.D. in Educational Administration. I wanted to become a school administrator. At NYU I learned a lot of things about administration, and I began to understand why some of my previous administrators had done certain things. I remembered the children complaining to me, but their words had never gotten through the superintendent's door. When I became an administrator I want to keep the door open.

Now I am traveling back and forth between New York and Philadelphia to do my administrative internship at the Pennsylvania School for the Deaf. My intern program is under the headmaster of the school. He has taught me many things about administrative policies, and I have become much more sensitive to the responsibilities of people in that area. I hope after I get my Ph.D. that I am going to become an administrator. When I do, I want to make things a lot better for the school where I work.

CHAPTER 8

Lessons Learned from My Elders

Frank R. Turk

As the director of Junior National Association of the Deaf (Jr. NAD), I naturally love young people, and I like to talk to them. Many young people have asked me this question, "When you were in school, from whom did you learn the most?" I have answered them, "Deaf adults." Young people are puzzled with this answer. They tell me they mean whom did I learn the most from when I was in school. Again I say, "Deaf adults taught me the most." They have looked at me and said, "You misunderstood us. We are talking about when you were small and in school." Then, they ask me which school I was in. I reply, "I attended the Minnesota School for the Deaf, MSD." "From whom did you learn the most at MSD?" they ask. Again, my answer is deaf adults. It's true that I learned more from deaf adults than from books, classroom lessons, or anything else. I will give you some examples of what deaf adults themselves taught me while I was growing up, things I still remember to this day.

One deaf adult, an old man, complained about the way I dressed. He noticed that I dressed the same way every day. Whether it was Monday, Tuesday, Wednesday, Thursday, or Friday, I always wore a white shirt and a tie. The old man didn't like that; he wanted to help me improve my appearance. He asked me, "Frank, why don't you have variety in your clothes?" I didn't understand what he meant.

"It's fine to wear a white shirt and tie on Monday," he said. "But Tuesday, why don't you wear something different? You could wear a bow tie and maybe a beige shirt. Then Wednesday, change to a different tie with a yellow shirt. Thursday, perhaps you could wear a blue shirt and maybe a bow tie again. Friday, it would be okay to go back to a white shirt and tie, or bow tie, or whatever you choose. Try wearing different clothes each day. Impress people with your variety of taste in clothes."

That adult taught me many things about clothes and appearance. I took his advice because I respected him.

About two weeks later, I bought a bow tie. Then I went to my room and tried to tie it. I tied it, but it didn't come out right. I took it off and tried to tie it again. It was hard, but I kept trying. Finally, I gave up. I went back to town and bought a bow tie with clips which fasten on the shirt collar. It was easier to put on because I didn't have to tie it. That kind of tie is for lazy people! I put it on and looked in the mirror. The tie looked nice. But I forgot one important thing. While clip ties are easy to put on, they also fall off easily. Whenever I signed to my teachers or friends, my tie began to fall off. I would clip it back on, but it would start to fall off again. This happened several times before I took the bow tie off and went back to a four-in-hand tie. Change to a bow tie? Forget it!

A few months later the old deaf man came back to school and looked me up. I was still Frank, but there was some improvement. I was wearing a beige shirt.

"Oh, I see you have a beige shirt," the man said to me. "Well, that is fine. What about the tie?"

I explained that I tried bow ties. One I couldn't tie, and the other one fell off.

He looked at me and asked, "How do you tie your shoe laces?"

I was disgusted that he would ask me a baby question like that. I knew how to tie my shoe laces.

He continued, "Do you know that you tie a bow tie the same way you tie your shoe laces?"

I didn't know that. I went to my room and stood in front of the mirror. I tied the bow tie like I tied my shoe laces. That was it. It worked! The old man taught me something that no one in school ever had time to teach me.

Another deaf adult taught me something important about hunting. He asked me, "When you are hunting on a windy day, do you hunt against the wind or with the wind?"

I explained that if it was a cold day and I faced the wind, my nose would freeze, so I would turn around. I hunted with the wind.

He said, "You never killed a deer, right?"

I replied, "That is right, but I try to improve."

"You are never going to improve," he said, "unless you suffer some." He explained that when you hunt with the wind, it is easy and comfortable for you, but you never see a deer. However, many deer see you and run away and hide. This happens because the wind carries your odor to the deer. When deer smell a human body, they run and the hunter doesn't see them.

I learned from that deaf adult that if I wanted to be a successful hunter, I had to hunt against the wind. If the deer don't know I am there, the chances are better that I will get a deer.

Another adult I remember very well asked me a question when I was about ten years old. He asked me to name the five Great Lakes. It is hard when you are young to remember their names. I told him that Lake Michigan was one. Then there was Lake Erie. But I wasted time trying to think of the other names. The adult asked me to spell the word homes. "H-o-m-e-s," I said.

"All right," he continued, "you can remember the five Great Lakes by putting the word homes in your mental file cabinet."

Now if you ask me the names of the five Great Lakes, I take the word homes out of my mental file cabinet and tell you, "*H*, Huron; *O*, Ontario; *M*, Michigan; *E*, Erie; *S*, Superior." That is an easy way to remember them. I learned many mental crutches from that adult. A mental crutch is a word you use to help you remember something. It is like using a crutch to help you walk when you break your leg.

I learned other mental crutch words from that adult. For example, the word faces helps me remember the five requirements for a person to be physically fit. The five requirements are: *F,* flexibility; *A,* agility; *C,* coordination; *E,* endurance; and *S,* strength. FACES! Oh, I have many memory crutch words in my mental file. If people ask me something, I use my crutch, and they think I'm smart. Really, I am clever. You don't have to be smart to do things like that. You just have to have the ideas; look for clever ways to remember things. I learned that from adults.

An interesting thing I learned from another adult was about accidents. One day the adult asked me, "If a person hit his head and was bleeding excessively, what would you do?"

I was small, and I looked at him and said, "I'd take off my shirt and wrap it around his head."

"Well, then what would you do?" he asked.

I said that I would telephone for an ambulance.

"No, you can't," he replied, "there are no hearing people here to make the call. So, what would you do?"

"My friend over there has a car," I said.

"Well, that is good," the adult said. "You put the man in the car to drive him to the hospital. Where is the hospital?"

"Oh, I know where it is. It is over there about four or five miles."

"Is that the road that leads to the hospital?" he asked me.

I told him that it was.

"What is the speed limit?" he wanted to know.

"It is 50 or 60 miles an hour, I guess," was my reply.

"Oh, no," he said. "It is 25 miles an hour. That is the speed limit. But do you have to drive that speed?"

I said, "No, I would go 50 or 60 miles an hour to save a life."

"You are right," he replied. "Now suppose a police car came up behind you with its siren on. What would you do?"

"I would show the police the injured man."

"No, you can't move or lift him," he continued. "You have to keep the man quiet. It is dangerous to move him."

"Well, I would pull over and stop," I said.

"You don't have time because the man is bleeding," the adult told me. "You have to hurry the hospital. He may be dying."

I said, "Maybe I could write a note to the police."

"If you try to write and drive at the same time, you could go in the ditch," he said.

"Oh, that is right. What do I do?"

My adult friend said, "It is easy. Roll down the window as you are driving. Wave anything white, like a handkerchief, at the police officer. The officer will understand that white means you want to go to the hospital. The police officer will pull in front of you and lead you to the hospital with the siren on."

I remembered that several years ago when one of my children got hurt. A pot of coffee spilled on his back. The pain was terrible. I put him in the car and started driving to the hospital. My son was screaming and crying. A police officer came along, so I rolled down the window and waved a white handkerchief. It worked; the police officer led me by the shortest route to the hospital. An adult taught me that, and it helped my son and me.

One adult I owe a lot to is Chester C. Dobson, my favorite teacher in school. When I was in school, I wanted most of all to have good

English language skills. You know that almost all deaf people want good language. If you have that, your friends will think you are a smart person. I knew people would respect me if I used good English. I wondered why it was so hard for me to master English. Why, for example, did I write and throw away piles of papers, but succeed in writing only one short sentence of four or five words? I felt dumb. I was afraid I was a hopeless case. My friends saw me writing and throwing papers out, maybe the three-hundredth draft of something. I didn't want them to think I was dumb.

I asked Mr. Dobson, my favorite teacher, why my language was so weak. His answer was, "Frank, you have too much pride. You are not willing to make mistakes in exchange for improvement."

I looked at him and said, "That's right, I really have a lot of pride, but I want to improve now."

He told me that I never took on leadership responsibilities in a club, the student body government, Junior NAD, or any similar group. I looked at him strangely; I didn't see any connection between holding office and acquiring good English. Then he explained that taking a leadership role would help improve my English. After he said that, I understood, so I decided to run for an office. I had to improve my language before I graduated. I had to be able to write, read, and understand well.

I asked my friend Marilyn to nominate me for president of the drama club. I wasn't skilled at drama, but I wanted to get the benefit of improving my language from leading a group, as Dr. Dobson had explained to me. My girlfriend said, "Okay, Saturday I will nominate you."

That was on Monday. Monday night I couldn't sleep; I tossed and turned. I was worried about my rival. In school all boys and girls have rivals competing for offices, like president of a club, for the best grades, for captain of the football or basketball team, or for getting the most points. How I disliked my rival. If I stood up as president and made a mistake, he would laugh and say, "Ha, you dumb cluck." No, I wasn't going to give him that opportunity. So I decided not to run for office.

Tuesday morning I met Marilyn and said, "Don't bring up my name Saturday. Drop it." But during the day my conscience bothered me. Mr. Dobson was right. I should be willing to make mistakes in exchange for learning. I met Marilyn again and said I still wanted her to nominate me on Saturday. Tuesday night I had another sleepless night, tossing and turning because of my rival. The next morning I told Marilyn again to drop it. Every day that week I changed my mind. I would tell her to nominate me; then I would tell her not to do it. Finally I decided to let her nominate me.

At the meeting my name was put on the chalkboard: Frank Turk. I looked at it and I was scared! I was hoping a lot of other students would be nominated, too. If I lost, I could always tell Mr. Dobson that I tried. That would be better than chickening out. But no one else was nominated, and I was elected president by acclamation.

Many names were listed on the board to be vice-president. There was a lot of arguing and excitement about that position, but I didn't pay any attention. I was busy thinking of what I would say to the club. They always asked the new president to make a few remarks or explain how he or she planned to improve things in the club. I had to think up some sentences to say. When the secretary and treasurer were elected, they called me, the new president, to go forward and say a few words. I wasn't scared when I got up because I had the words and sentences in my head. I walked to the stage, started up the steps, and fell! All the words I had thought of fell out of my mind; they disappeared! I stood up and left.

The next year I volunteered for a different office, but the same thing happened. I sat there, wrestling with words to say. Talking in front of people still bothered me, but I didn't want it to bother me. I started walking up the steps and fell again. Most of the words left me, but I kept one or two that time, so I had a few to start with. I was improving a little bit. The following year I volunteered for another office. I saw the faces of the people around me, and then I realized that we were all the same. I knew I had improved during the past year. Now if I fell, everything would stay in my mind. It wouldn't make any difference; it was like the words were taped in my mind.

Mr. Dobson taught me that leadership can be your best twenty-four-hour a day teacher. I understood that to lead a group successfully you must first be a clear thinker. Clear thinking requires good language, and good language requires planning and practice. For example, if I have to speak somewhere now, I plan the speech and practice it the night before. I go over what I am going to say again and again. The next day I can give the speech smoothly. That was what Mr. Dobson meant. By volunteering to take active roles in organizations, you have opportunities to develop better language. That can be your best English teacher.

Bar Talk

Jack R. Gannon

Do you know who B.B.B. is? B.B.B. is Byron B. Burns. He was the president of the National Association of the Deaf for many years—eighteen years in a row, I think. Let me tell you a short funny story about him.

One day B.B.B. decided to stop by a local bar after work to have a drink. He was tired and wanted to sit down and rest a bit. He entered the bar, walked up to the counter, and sat down. Noticing a man next to him, B.B.B. took out his pencil and pad and started to write. He introduced himself to the man, and they began a nice conversation. After awhile another hearing man came in and sat down next to B.B.B. B.B.B. felt this man should be included also, so he wrote back and forth between the two men. B.B.B. was deaf and the other two men were hearing, but they got along just fine. The three of them had a good conversation with pad and pencil.

Later B.B.B. looked at his watch. Wow! It was getting late! It was best for him to go home; his wife was waiting for him. He wrote, "Excuse me, I have to go now. I enjoyed talking with both of you. Good-bye."

As he was going out the door, B.B.B. looked back. He saw that the two hearing men were still writing notes back and forth to each other. B.B.B. shrugged his shoulders and left.

CHAPTER 9

Through an Act of God

Deborah M. Sonnenstrahl

I want to share a true story with you. It is about a famous sculptor who lived in the nineteenth century, quite a while ago. His name was Daniel Chester French. He made two famous statues. One is the Gallaudet Group. It is a statue of Thomas H. Gallaudet, father of Dr. Edward Gallaudet, who was the first president of Gallaudet College. The statue shows Thomas Gallaudet sitting and holding a deaf girl, his first student. He is teaching her the first letter of the alphabet. His arm is around the girl and she is looking up at him, making the letter "A." It is a very impressive statue. The other statue Mr. French made was the Abraham Lincoln Memorial in Washington, D.C. It shows Lincoln sitting with his arms on the arms of a chair. It is very popular in Washington; many tourists visit the Memorial every year.

But let's go back to the Gallaudet statue. When Dr. Gallaudet was president of Gallaudet College, he and the alumni group asked Mr. French, the sculptor, to sculpt the statue of Thomas Gallaudet. Mr. French thought it over. He had never had any association with deafness. He had heard a lot about the wonderful things Gallaudet College was doing with deaf people. So he visited Gallaudet College and looked over the beautiful campus and its buildings. He walked all around. Then he said, "I think I will accept the job. I accept the commission." Everyone was excited and very happy because Mr. French was already a well-known sculptor.

People asked the sculptor where he was going to put the statue. Mr. French said, "I will have to walk around the campus once more just to make sure that I pick the right location for the statue."

One beautiful day he walked over the campus—the front, the back, and even in the fields. He walked along Florida Avenue, the street in front of Gallaudet College. He looked and made notes. He looked some more and made several sketches. Then he went to Dr. Gallaudet and told him, "I have the perfect place for the Gallaudet statue."

"Really?"

"Yes!"

"Where?"

Mr. French said, "Exactly in front of the college itself, facing the college with the back to Florida Avenue where people passing by can glance at it."

The alumni thought it was the perfect place, right in the center of everything. However, a few people on campus were unhappy. The unhappy people were Dr. Gallaudet's children. You must remember that in the past and even today, some of the college's presidents have lived on campus in a big house. Dr. Gallaudet and his family lived on campus. His children played on campus and also played with the students. Everyone knew each other very well.

The children were unhappy about the place chosen for the statue because that location had a large and beautiful tree, an oak tree, I think. Its trunk and limbs were thick. The tree was very old; it had seen many, many days. The children had a swing in the tree. This place was their favorite playground. But Mr. French, that mean old man, wanted to put the statue right in the middle of their play area. That meant someone would have to cut the tree down. That was unheard of! What a terrible thing! That tree was their beloved playmate. It protected the children from rain, and on warm days they sat beneath it in its cool shade. The sculptor was going to kill a friend! The children ran home. They argued with their parents. They told Dr. Gallaudet, "You can't do that to us; you can't, you can't, you can't!"

Dr. Gallaudet, like all good fathers, didn't want to hurt his children. As president of Gallaudet College, he had to think of some way to solve the problem. He was torn between the alumni group and his children. So he told the alumni group, the children, and Mr. French,

"Let me think it over. Let me sleep on it." That poor man! He had a burden on his shoulders. He went home and got ready for bed.

During the night there was a terrible storm—lightning, thunder, and rain. It rained all night. In the middle of the night the family heard something—a very loud thump! Dr. Gallaudet looked out the window, and do you know what? The tree was hit by lightning!

The result was that Mr. French was happy. The alumni group was happy. Were the children happy? No, no, no! But through an act of God, Mr. French got his wish.

Sink or Swim

Michael Schwartz

When I was a small boy in Chicago living with my family, every weekend we'd go to the swimming pool at a high school in that city. There was a swimming instructor at the pool. I wasn't permitted to go into the deep end of the swimming pool—never in the deep end because all the big boys played there. I was only allowed to stay in the shallow end where the little children stayed.

One day, I remember it very well, my parents were watching me, a group of other children, and the teacher. I was so excited that I swam with my head under water without really looking to see where I was going. I continued to swim and it was great! I swam and swam, and when I stopped, I found myself in the deep end of the pool.

At that moment I looked up and saw my mother. She was panicked. I had to think fast. I was in the deep end of the pool where everyone had told me I couldn't swim. I was taking lessons in the shallow end so that I could learn how to swim, but here I was in the deep end of the pool. I took a deep breath and swam all the way back to the other end of the pool. I got there safely, and my mother was so relieved. I thought to myself that everyone had told me I couldn't swim there, but when the moment came and I had to swim, I did.

Now I'm a student at New York University School of Law. I remember that before going to NYU, I said to myself, "I can't do it. It will be too much work for me." Then I thought of my earlier experience. I pictured swimming to the deep end of the pool, being stuck, and swimming back. I did it! Here I am in school and doing well. I just *thought* that I couldn't do the work at NYU. What is the moral of the story? You can do whatever you need to do. It really is possible!

How I Lied My Way to the Bottom

Thomas A. Mayes

Deaf people always have a very difficult time finding work in professional fields. As I look back at my younger days when I was first out of college, I recall such experiences. I think sometimes that time stands still.

When I graduated from the University of Chicago, I started out to look for work. My goal was to become an advertising copywriter. I quickly learned some hard facts of business life, including the fact that advertising people did not have an open heart for deaf individuals. The largest national advertising agencies in Chicago were located in tall buildings on North Michigan Boulevard, so I went to the Palmolive Building and took an elevator up to the top floor. I started with an agency called Batten, Barton, Durstein and Osborne. That company was and is very famous because when we say that name it sounds like a trunk falling down the stairs.

I went to the office of the Personnel Manager. He looked at me, the first deaf person he ever met, and said to himself, "My Lord, what a lot of nerve!" Then he got himself together and said, "Young man, how much experience have you had?"

I replied, "None really. I just graduated from college, but I am young, full of energy and ready to work."

"I'm afraid we can't take you," he said. "In this business we always look for experienced people. I'm sorry. Try something else."

So I moved down floor by floor and got the same reaction from other agencies. By the time I came to the fourth floor, I decided to lie a little bit. I said, "Well, I had two years experience working in small businesses writing advertisements." It didn't work, so I lied a little bit more about my experience—four years, five years, and so on. By the time I hit the ground floor, I was really the most polished liar to ever graduate from the University of Chicago.

What I Learned about Irish Sign Language

Bernard Bragg

What I enjoyed most about my world tour a few years ago was learning foreign sign languages. They all look different. I learned Russian, Finnish, Swedish, Norwegian, Irish, and Spanish sign languages—I visited twenty-five different countries. I found I was able to learn sign language very quickly. Also, I found that I was able to completely erase the one I had just learned from my mind just as quickly so I could learn another foreign sign language when I moved on.

I remember when I arrived in Dublin, Ireland, I met a very nice young couple, a married couple, who offered to show me around town. That was fine. We spent the whole day visiting the big, beautiful town of Dublin. The husband drove the car, and the wife sat next to him so she could point out the different sights to me. I sat in the back seat. As she described the sights to me, I learned sign language at the same time.

Every so often the husband and wife would criticize each other saying, "No, you're wrong. You're using the wrong sign." They would go back and forth. I became confused. Who was right? Then I asked them, "How long have you been married?"

"Oh," they replied, "seven years."

"That's long enough to be able to communicate with each other without any great difficulty," I said. "Why then do you keep on disagreeing about signs? I don't understand."

The wife explained to me the reason why their sign languages were not exactly the same. They came from two different schools. Oh, I could understand then why they sometimes disagreed, especially when the two schools were probably far apart. That would explain why their signs would be that much different. But, no, that was not true. They told me their schools were in the same town and that they were within walking distance of each other. Yet their sign languages were tremendously different. I asked them to explain to me how that happened.

The wife said, "Well, one school was run by nuns for girls only. The other school was run by the Christian Brothers for boys only. For over 150 years the Christian Brothers and the nuns were not on speaking terms. They were not friendly with each other. If they met, they both looked the other way. That explains why their sign languages became increasingly different."

It was really sad. What a shame! Can you imagine how the boys and girls felt when they finished school, met each other, and started to talk, only to find out that they couldn't understand each other? The wife told me that it was not until about four years before that they finally set up a committee to develop one sign language. They chose a few people to help unify the two different sign languages into one that could be used all over the country. They selected some signs from the girls' school, some signs from the boys' school, and then they modified the signs a little. They put these signs in a book called *The Unified Sign Language.* They published the book and distributed it to the two schools and to other schools in Ireland. Now everyone is happy.

After explaining this the wife asked me, "Do you know what we call this sign language now?"

"No, what?" I asked.

"Unisex Language!" she replied.

Impossible Dream?

Thomas A. Mayes

I grew up in the state of Oregon, way out west. When I was about sixteen years old, I came to Washington, D.C., to attend a Boy Scout Jamboree. It was a wonderful experience for young boys from the farm country. We camped across the Potomac River in an area that I would guess now is the LBJ Memorial Grove. There were several thousand of us there. One day I read in the camp paper that Dr. Percival Hall, President of Gallaudet College, had invited the deaf Scouts to the campus for a picnic and a chance to socialize.

The picnic was on Hotchkiss Field. There were about thirty of us. We had a wonderful time talking and getting to know each other. I also had the opportunity to shake hands and talk with the second president of Gallaudet College.

At that age all of us youngsters had big aspirations for ourselves. I asked Dr. Hall if it was possible for a deaf person to earn a doctorate. Dr. Hall, instead of asking why not, which is the appropriate thing to say these days, asked why. He said it was hard enough for deaf people to get a B.A. degree.

Gallaudet and I

Nancy Rarus

When the doctor told me that my baby was deaf, I looked at my son and made the letter "A." The baby was just crawling, but in my mind, a vision unfolded—a vision from the past of a man named Thomas Hopkins Gallaudet and a little girl named Alice. Alice was a small deaf girl who had never been to school. Many years ago there were no schools for deaf children. Families often locked them in mental institutions, and hid them away in shame. Gallaudet, who was a minister, was walking along one day when he saw the little girl playing. He had heard talk among the neighbors that something was wrong with her. She was deaf. He tapped Alice on the shoulder, and she looked up at him. Mr. Gallaudet wanted to help her. He taught her how to write the word, h-a-t. This was her first word, hat! Alice was excited; she ran to her father, a rich doctor.

The doctor noticed Gallaudet's real interest in Alice and her deafness. Friends and rich neighbors of the doctor in Hartford, Connecticut, talked among themselves and decided to send Thomas Gallaudet to England. This was back around 1815. They had heard that there was a school for deaf people in England. Perhaps Gallaudet could learn how to set up such a school in the United States for Alice and others who were deaf.

Mr. Gallaudet went to England, but he got nothing there, no help at all. When he asked why the teachers would not tell him anything, they said that their method of teaching the deaf was a family secret. He went on to Scotland, but he received the same answer. Teachers wouldn't help him. Gallaudet did learn that students there were not allowed to sign; the teachers slapped their hands if they tried. Speech (oralism) was emphasized. The teachers in Scotland told Gallaudet that he had better go to France.

Thomas Gallaudet went to France and found sign language being used. Do you know how the French people learned sign language? They learned from the priests. In the past, the monks taught the deaf children of very rich families. The monks developed a way to communicate with deaf children in sign language. This method was brought from Italy to France. Gallaudet found a school for the deaf in France which he went to visit.

Abbé Sicard, the head of the school, met Mr. Gallaudet and was very happy to show him how the deaf were taught in the school. He also introduced Gallaudet to Laurent Clerc. Clerc was deaf. "Clerc can show you how to teach the deaf," the Abbé said. So Mr. Gallaudet stayed in France. He learned that Mr. Clerc was a fine man, and he was tempted to steal Clerc away from the school. He did ask Clerc to go to America with him. Mr. Clerc thought about it, and finally Gallaudet convinced him. Abbé Sicard was disappointed, but he agreed to let Clerc go for a short time. However, Laurent Clerc never went back to teach in France again.

Thomas Gallaudet returned to the United States with Clerc. They established a school for the deaf in Hartford, Connecticut, with seven children. One of them was Alice. That happened way back in 1817.

Researchers have learned from some old papers that Alice felt isolated as a deaf child. She felt uncomfortable around hearing people. She felt the same way many deaf people feel today. Once Alice wrote a letter to a friend complaining that her mother forced her to go to tea. "I hate to go to tea, sipping, and watching the hearing ladies gossip," she said. "I feel isolated. I would rather stay home alone; it would be better." It is the same now; it is still true for many deaf people.

Mr. Gallaudet, a hearing man, married a deaf woman named Sophia Fowler. They had several children, several hearing children. Theirs was the first deaf-hearing marriage that is documented. Today, there are many marriages between deaf and hearing people.

Now I look at my son who is deaf. I think of Thomas Gallaudet teaching Alice the letter "A." I begin to teach my son "A."

.

CHAPTER 10

The Sonic Boom of 1994

Mervin D. Garretson

Back in the 1970s there was an airplane called the *Supersonic Concorde*. This plane could fly from New York to England or France in three hours. The speed was called Mach 2, which meant the plane traveled about 1,300 miles an hour.

People in the United States were still not happy or satisfied with this speed. Many business people and government people wanted to cross the Atlantic Ocean in just one hour. If they could fly to Paris or London in one hour, then they could live there and work here, or live here and work there. It would be much easier to commute back and forth and much faster. Also, the people of France, England, and the United States could share their ideas and cultures.

The U.S. government thought about this idea for a while. Then it gave a great deal of money to the aircraft industry to investigate, analyze, and develop an even better plane than the Concorde. This job took many years of planning and at least two full years of production work.

May 1, 1994, was a very important day in the United States—the new plane (the SSC-F4) was completed. This ultrasonic plane could fly to England in only one hour. That was really FAST. People flocked to the John F. Kennedy airport in New York to see the new plane. Newspaper reporters, radio and TV people, business people, and high government officials all converged at the airport to watch the new SSC-F4 take off.

United States President Jackson Graves sat in the Oval Office at the White House with his cabinet members and watched a huge TV screen. Workers in factories, hospitals, schools, and colleges all had the day off to watch TV and see the big ultrasonic plane take off. All over the United States, and even other parts of the world, people were watching TV.

When the time came, the plane opened its jets and roared into the sky. The power seemed equal to 100 Boeing-747 airplanes. The plane zoomed off fast. In just a few seconds it reached the speed of sound. (The speed of sound is called the sound barrier.) When the plane broke the sound barrier it made a loud noise—a sonic boom. Such a sonic boom had never happened before. Every person in the United States heard this boom. They continued to sit and watch their TV sets as the plane went up into the sky.

President Graves looked around the room at his cabinet members. He had a big smile on his face. He said, "Our experiment with the new airplane seems very successful. The takeoff was beautiful." The cabinet members looked at the president strangely, saying nothing. The president looked around the room again and said, "Our experiment seems very successful, right?"

The cabinet members continued to stare at him. Finally, the Secretary of Health said, "Excuse me, Mr. President, but we can't understand you."

Now it was the president who was looking at him, saying, "I don't understand you."

All of the cabinet members suddenly began talking and looking around at each other in a frightened way. They could not hear each other. It was all very confusing. One cabinet member picked up a telephone and dialed, but she heard no sound. She hung up, still wondering what was going on.

The Secretary of Health wrote a note and handed it to the president. "It seems we all have temporary deafness from that sonic boom. We had better call the White House doctor." The cabinet members and the president agreed. They sat and waited for the message to get to the doctor.

While the president sat in the Oval Office, the vice-president sat in a meeting in the U.S. Senate. Everyone looked up at him, but they didn't understand a word. When the senators realized they could not hear each other, they became frightened. Things became very confusing and everyone panicked. The senators were really scared; they began to gesture and yell. After a while a telex came in from government officials. The telex said that all men, women, and children in the United States had become totally deaf from the sonic boom. They were shocked.

What had happened to the country? The United States had become a nation of deaf people. There was not one hearing person left in the United States, only deaf people. In the department stores and other business places, clerks used big pads of paper so people could write notes. Radio sales and related businesses went down. People turned on their television sets, but they could not hear anything and they became discouraged. Telephone operators sat back and didn't work all day. Telephones did not ring. The operators just sat and drank coffee all day. Once in a while they would get a switchboard call through the TTY. But other than that, it was a very quiet country. People didn't know what to do or how to handle their deafness.

The president of the National Association of the Deaf (NAD) called his board members on the TTY to set up a meeting in Washington, D.C. The NAD board members, who had always been deaf, flew in from all parts of the country for the meeting. The NAD president announced, "We had better have a meeting with people at the White House. We need to help our country."

All agreed he was right. They sent a telegram to the president of the United States. President Graves read the telegram that explained the NAD would be happy to help: "We've lived with deafness all our lives and you are kind of confused by it."

The president of the United States became excited. He sent a wire back to the NAD saying, "Please, do come and help us out."

All of the cabinet members came to the White House to meet with the NAD president and his board. They were aware of how easy it was for the NAD board members to sign back and forth, while they slowly wrote notes back and forth to each other. The U.S. president commented on how fast the NAD people could communicate.

At the end of the meeting, President Graves announced that the NAD should set up a national program for teaching sign language to all the people of the country. So, the NAD selected skilled deaf teachers to teach the newly deafened population. At colleges, schools, and businesses everywhere, people began to learn sign language.

The job market improved for deaf people already fluent in sign language. The others were out of luck; even the interpreters could not hear! People removed their car radios and replaced them with TV screens. They also removed their car horns and installed lights like on an ambulance or fire truck. Things changed all over the United States in many different ways.

In the fall it came time for the national elections. People who had been deaf all their lives and were skilled in signing turned out to be the best speakers. They won victories over those who had just lost their hearing and were inept at signs or knew no signs at all. So, one deaf person became governor of Maryland and another became governor of California. And, finally, in the ultimate contest, Tim O'Hara, president of the NAD, was nominated for president of the United States. He won by a landslide. And that is how we got our first deaf president of the United States.

1776: Deaf People's Contributions

Roslyn Rosen

We all know the United States is a free country today. We also know that more than two hundred years ago, American colonists fought to gain independence from England. But, do you know how it really started? Do you know how deaf people helped to fight and win freedom for America? Let me tell you.

My great, great, great, great-grandfather was born on Martha's Vineyard (near Boston, Massachusetts) in 1730. His name was Silence Dogood. At that time, many deaf people lived on Martha's Vineyard, more than in other parts of the country. Usually there is about one deaf person for each one thousand hearing people. But, on Martha's Vineyard there was 1 deaf person for each 155 hearing people. The hearing people accepted deafness as a natural thing. They signed and used total communication; there was no problem. When my great, great, great, great-grandfather Silence Dogood lived, the United States was not a country yet; it was still thirteen colonies under the rule of the English government.

You might know a famous man who lived at that time—Ben Franklin. He was a famous inventor, printer, scientist, and politician. He met my great, great, great, great-grandfather and became fascinated with him. They wrote notes back and forth. Ben hired Silence Dogood to work with him. Ben did not really have a good education when he was growing up. But writing notes back and forth with my great, great, great, great-grandfather helped Ben to become a skilled writer. Ben started writing articles for newspapers, but he felt people wouldn't really pay attention to him. So, he used the name Dogood as his pen name.

My great, great, great, great-grandfather worked with Ben Franklin in his print shop and they wrote the newspaper, the *Pennsylvania Gazette*. After a while, Ben decided to hire more deaf people. Writing notes gave him a really good idea; it made him think about establishing a post office so that everyone could send notes. And that's how the post office system got started in the United States. In those days, the United States was under the control of the English Parliament (government). Parliament tried to increase taxes. The colonists became angry because they were not allowed to vote. Parliament sent British soldiers to the colonies to make sure that the colonists did not fight or complain. One day in Boston in 1770, a colonist tried to get a soldier's attention. The soldier did not respond, so the colonist threw a rock at the soldier. British soldiers immediately shot into the crowds and killed five citizens and wounded seven.

When that news reached Ben Franklin, he said, "We have to put it right into the newspaper, that the British soldiers killed our people." But Ben was in a real hurry; he didn't have time to write the story down. So he just told the deaf printer, "Five people were killed and seven wounded by the British." The deaf printer prepared the headline, "5,700 People Killed in Boston Massacre!" The newspaper was printed and distributed. Ben Franklin returned to the shop, saw that headline, and said to the deaf printer, "No, that's wrong! I said 5, not 5,700! You're fired!"

Many people who saw the newspaper became very angry. Before, they had thought, "Oh, so what, we don't mind paying a little bit of tax. No big deal." But, when the Boston Massacre happened, they started to get real upset. They wanted to be free from English rule. So they all gathered at the print shop and they said, "Ben Franklin, you're right about the British. We want to join the army. We can fight. We'll work together to be free." Then they all left.

Ben Franklin then said, "This is great. I won't tell them it was a mistake. We want them to unite." The deaf printer said with relief, "Okay, but we need to communicate better. Can you learn sign language?" Ben Franklin replied, "Okay." So, he learned to sign a little bit. But it was really hard for him because it was so cold. Ben Franklin then invented the pot-bellied stove. And that's why the pot-bellied stove was invented—to keep the hands warm for signing!

More and more people in the colonies started communicating with each other. They stood outside, talking and talking about the English control over the colonies. The English soldiers objected. They made it illegal for groups to assemble in public. Talking was not allowed! But you know you can't stop deaf people from talking on street corners. They just ignored the English. They talked among themselves and shared news such as "Do you know what happened? The English are going to increase our taxes. They're going to tax our tea."

People started to complain. They didn't think that Parliament should increase taxes. "We have no voice. We object to taxation without representation. If they want to tax us, fine. But let us vote for it and support it or reject it. So, what should we do about it?" One colonist said, "Why don't we dress as Indians, sneak onto the English ship, and throw the crates of tea into Boston Harbor?" So a group of colonists went to the ship and threw the crates of tea into Boston Harbor. The Boston Tea Party started the deaf people and hearing people working together. Hearing people looked up to deaf people in Boston. They were brave, rebelling against English rule. News of the Boston Tea Party arrived at Congress and made them announce war against England.

Ben Franklin heard that Congress supported war against England to free the colonies. He ran to his print shop late, late at night in the rain and cold. Ben didn't care, he wanted to get that headline, "America at War against England," into the paper. When he got to his print shop, he couldn't find his key. He remembered that his deaf assistant had a key. He went to his assistant's home that dark, cloudy night. He banged on the door but got no response. (At this time there were no doorbells or flashing lights for deaf people.) Ben was really stuck. He needed that key to open his print ship. Then he saw a light on the second floor. That meant the deaf assistant was in bed in that room.

Ben thought of a plan. He got a big red kite. He let it up and tried to get it in front of his assistant's window. The deaf man noticed the kite, stuck his head out of the window, and saw Ben. "What do you want? It's midnight." Ben slowly signed, "I need key." The deaf man said, "I have the key, but I don't want to walk all the way downstairs. So, I'll just tie the key to the kite string. Okay?" Ben said, "Okay."

So the deaf man grabbed the string and tied the big iron key onto the string. Just at that same moment the clouds broke open and lightning shot down and struck the key. The shock traveled down to Ben Franklin and he said, "I discovered electricity!" But we know that was really a deaf man's discovery.

Deaf people really communicated well with each other during the Revolution. (You know how fast the news travels through the deaf grapevine.) They were good at getting out information and news about what was happening with the colonies and with the English. The American soldiers became known as Minutemen. That meant soldiers and communicators. The hearing and deaf soldiers worked together. Paul Revere was perhaps the best known Minuteman. He rode on his horse through the towns letting people know what was going on.

One night the British soldiers were going to attack. The colonists didn't want to be surprised because they didn't have enough guns, bullets, or cannons. They didn't have many soldiers, but the British had many, many soldiers. The colonists didn't know which areas to protect. They had no idea if the British were coming by sea on a ship, or by land on horses. Paul Revere said, "It doesn't matter. Someone can give me a signal. I'll just let you know, and then you can get together in the right way to protect yourselves."

Nearby, there was a big church with a big bell. But Paul Revere could not hear, he was deaf himself. So, they used lights to give him the signal—"one if by land, two if by sea." When Paul Revere saw the number of lights, he rode his horse through the town to warn the soldiers and the Minutemen. The British could not beat the colonists, and no one died in that battle. In Concord, Massachusetts, there is a famous statue of a Minuteman standing with a gun. [By the way, the person who made that statue was Daniel Chester French. He also made the famous statue of Abraham Lincoln in the Lincoln Memorial in Washington, D.C. If you look at that statue of Lincoln, you will see that his hands carry his initials—A.L. Daniel Chester French also made the statue of Thomas Gallaudet showing Alice Cogswell the handshape for the letter A. That shows you that the statues of Lincoln, Gallaudet, and the Minuteman are all related to deafness.]

The famous battle of Bunker Hill was fought in 1775. You probably know about that battle. The colonists had several problems— not enough guns, not enough bullets, and not enough soldiers. There were only fifteen hundred American soldiers. They were inexperienced. They were farmers, printers, and so on. They were up against three thousand professional British soldiers who had plenty of experience and training. At Bunker Hill the American soldiers became nervous as they watched and waited for the British soldiers. Nothing happened. The deaf soldiers started talking and signing to each other. All of a sudden, they looked up—the British soldiers were almost on top of them! They grabbed their guns and fired. That really impressed General Gage. He said, "Wow, deaf soldiers really save ammunition. Okay, from now on the rule is: Do not fire until you see the whites of the enemies' eyes!"

Tom Jefferson traveled through the colonies to see what was going on. He explained to the people that he wanted the thirteen colonies to become a free country. Tom Jefferson didn't know sign language. He had a difficult time communicating with deaf people, and deaf people had a hard time understanding him. Finally, he had to write everything down to explain what he meant. That paper became the Declaration of Independence. Jefferson wrote that famous paper in 1776. It was really written for the benefit of deaf people. But now, it's a very, very important paper for all Americans.

The colonists continued fighting battles with the British. They won another battle in 1777, the battle of Saratoga. Deaf people were thrilled. They were puzzled why Ben Franklin looked so unhappy. "What's the matter with you? We've won! You should be happy." Ben replied, "Oh I'm worried about the future. What will happen to us? We're using up all our guns and bullets. Our cannons are falling apart, and our soldiers are dying off. We don't have enough of anything. We really need to win this war. I've already gone to France several times, but . . ." And the deaf people said, "But what? What? What?" Ben said, "I just can't communicate with the French. They can't understand me."

My great, great, great, great-grandfather, Silence Dogood, said, "I'll go with you. I'll be your interpreter. I'm great at interpreting with other people in other languages. I'll have no problem." Ben cheered up and said, "Why not? We must have help from the French." Ben and Silence sailed to France and met with the government representatives and the deaf people there. My great, great, great, great-grandfather signed to a deaf Frenchman who then spoke French to the French government officials. The government officials said, "Now we understand. We didn't understand what you wanted before. We will be happy to give money, supplies, and soldiers." Later, Ben and Silence went to Spain to talk to the king. With deaf people interpreting, they influenced the king to help, too. The king said, "I'll help America fight against England."

England became very weak. The rest is history. You know the colonists won the war, they won their freedom. But the question is: Could the United States of America have become a free country without the help of deaf people?

CHAPTER 11

February 3rd

Carl N. Schroeder

On February 3rd the radio, TV, and newspaper people became very excited. There was a big announcement that someone had seen an unidentified flying object (UFO) through a telescope. This UFO was headed straight for Earth. Everybody went crazy. Nobody knew what was going on. Was it really a UFO? Why was it coming to Earth? No one knew.

Everybody began talking about this UFO. Everyone watched the news to find out what was happening. Someone reported seeing a white flag on the UFO. A white flag was a truce symbol: it meant one side wanted to stop a conflict. No one knew what this white flag meant. Many different people, including religious leaders and politicians, got into great discussions about this. What would happen to Earth? Nobody knew the answer.

The spaceship moved closer and closer to Earth. All of the world leaders—the presidents, the kings, the queens, the princes, even the Russians—got together to talk about the UFO. They asked questions like, What was going on with this UFO? Was it a spy ship? Could it be from another planet? Was there really life out there?

The leaders did not know what to think, but they kept watching. All of a sudden the UFO stopped! Then, just as suddenly, all of the people—deaf people and hearing people—heard a voice. All of them understood it. The voice said that all the kings and queens, the pope, the religious leaders, and the political leaders must come to the UFO. But how? How could they get to it?

The president of the United States said, "Oh, we have space shuttles. We have plenty of them. We can send all of the leaders up to the UFO."

All the shuttles took off and went to the UFO. The UFO was huge. All of the space shuttles could land on it. The kings and queens and all of the leaders got out of the shuttles and went inside the UFO. They did not see anybody in the UFO, but they heard something that made them look up. There was a great big rectangle and a voice was speaking. It was speaking through this rectangle. It was not a loudspeaker. No, it was the rectangle itself, welcoming these people to the UFO called *White Flag UFO*. "We want to commend you for your wonderful work in behalf of your countries and for Earth. We want you to give us your recollections. Each of you tell a little bit about your country."

The kings and queens, the presidents, and the pope were all amazed; they were really honored. They each told a little bit about how they served their people.

Then, the voice said, "Now you must face the questions of the Council of Rectangles."

All the leaders went into a great big council room. Instead of people, the room was full of rectangles; each rectangle was a different color. The rectangles were arranged in a semicircle. They asked very intelligent questions. These rectangles asked about peace and war and love and hate—really high-level, abstract, important questions. After the question session, the Council of Rectangles began discussing something, but the Earth leaders could not understand what the rectangles were saying.

Suddenly the council announced that only two people had answered questions well—the pope and the very young princess. "These two will now go back to Earth," the council said. "All of the others of you will have to be punished. You are going to be taken out of here." So the pope and the young princess were flown back down to Earth, and the UFO took off. No one knew where it went—it just took off, disappearing within a second. The pope and the princess were really sad, naturally.

When the pope and the princess landed back on Earth, no one came to get them out of the shuttle. Nobody! So they opened the door by themselves. As they opened it up and walked off the shuttle they realized that there had been a nuclear war. When all of the leaders had gone up to the UFO, the people on Earth had pushed the panic button and destroyed everything. And so these two were the only two people left on Earth. They looked at each other; could they be the new Adam and Eve?

Fire in a Tree

H. Paul Menkis

One evening a father was sitting in the living room. His little daughter came up to him, sat on his lap, and said, "Daddy, tell me a story."

The father said, "What story do you want me to tell you?"

The little girl said, "I don't know, you choose a story."

The father said, "I really don't know what story to tell you."

The little girl looked around the room. Then, she noticed the fire in the fireplace. "Tell me how the fire burns from the wood," she said.

The father thought about that for a few minutes and said, "Okay. I know how I'll explain it to you. Ready?"

The little girl nodded her head. She was all ears and all eyes.

The father began, "A long, long time ago, that wood you see there was a large tree. Prior to that, the tree was as small as you. And before that, it was merely a seed. It had been dropped into the soil, watered by the rain, and nourished by the soil, and it had grown bigger and bigger. One day the tree branches sprouted leaves. The leaves absorbed the sunlight, and the sunlight filtered down into the rest of the tree. While that happened, the tree grew wider and taller, and many more branches grew out of it.

"Over the years the tree absorbed a lot of sunlight. The sun is very far away. Now suppose a tree were to touch the sun, what would happen? The tree would burn up! But even from far away, the sunlight nourishes the tree. The tree absorbs all the heat, which filters down into the roots. The tree stores the heat for many, many years. Later, when the tree gets old or people need the tree, someone chops it down and cuts into logs. You know, logs just like the ones we have right here in the fireplace.

"Now, those logs, or wood any place, can be lit by striking a match and holding it to the wood. The match makes the wood wake up. It comes to life; it burns. Now what does all this mean? That wood, which has been taking in the heat from the sun year after year, has been waiting for you. All you need to do is strike a match. When the wood catches on fire, it gives you that heat from the sun. And that's how we get fire."

The little girl was fascinated with this. She thought about it as she walked off to bed. She continued to think about it. How interesting it was—taking in the heat and giving us warmth. How wonderful it was that trees did that for us.

The little girl fell asleep. The next morning the sun on her face woke her up. Immediately she thought of the trees. She got out of bed and dressed quickly. Then she ran outside and looked in awe at the trees. She touched one, she hugged it, and she kissed it.

The Chalk

Carl N. Schroeder

I died and my soul went up to heaven. I walked up to the golden gate and tried to open it, but it was locked. I noticed a doorbell, so I pressed the doorbell and I waited and waited—I waited a long time. I couldn't really see much through the gate because there was a hill. I became really curious about what was on the other side. I waited a long time by the gate. It seemed really strange that no one answered, so again I pushed the button. I waited and waited until finally an old man walked up. He had a long white beard. I didn't know what to do, so I just stood there. I waited until the old man came up and said, "May I help you?"

I answered, "Yes, I just died and now I'm here."

The old man said, "Oh! What is your name?"

I fingerspelled, "J-o-h-n K-o-l-a-t-a."

He said, "But I don't know your name."

So I said, "Who are you?"

"I'm Peter."

"Oh, I've heard of you down on earth. You're very famous."

"Yes, but I really don't know you."

"You don't know me?"

"No, I don't know who you are."

"But, I just died a little while ago and now I'm a soul. You're not expecting me?"

Peter said, "No. What is your name again?"

So I fingerspelled again, "J-o-h-n K-o-l-a-t-a."

"I don't know you."

"I'm shocked," I said. "There must be a mistake."

He said, "Yes, it must be a mistake. Well, let's see . . . I have a book that lists all people's lives. It's in my house. Why don't you come with me into the house."

That was fine with me. Peter opened the gates and we walked in. It smelled so good, just like the morning dew, like sweet flowers, I thought as we walked. Then we went into the house. There were rows and rows of books on the wall. The old man stood near the books and asked, "What is your name again?" I spelled Kolata. He found the book and asked, "What year were you born?" I told him, and then he looked for my name, but he couldn't find it. He wanted to know where I was born so I explained, but he still couldn't find it. Finally, he said, "I don't know who you are."

"What do you mean you don't know me?"

"I'm sorry," he said as he closed the book and put it back.

I said, "There must be a mistake. What's wrong?"

Peter said, "Well, have you ever sinned?"

"Well, I thought I was forgiven for all my sins, but . . ."

"Well, you can be forgiven. I will tell you how." And then he brought me some chalk, a great big piece of chalk. He explained, "Now with this chalk you have to make Xs for all the sins you ever committed. Put the Xs on the steps outside of the gate."

"You mean Xs on all the steps?"

He answered yes. So I went outside and Peter said, "Good luck and make sure you get all of your sins taken care of before you come back."

"Okay, I responded. I thought about my sins and I made one X. Then I remembered another sin, made another X, and on and on all the way down this long staircase. I made Xs and Xs that went on forever. And then I saw an old friend. He was walking toward me.

I wondered what he was doing walking up the stairs. I didn't really want him to notice me. I was sort of embarrassed about what I was doing. I tried to hide myself, but on these stairs there was absolutely no place to hide; I was stuck. So I went up to him and I asked, "Oh, what are you doing?"

He looked at me and said, "Well, how are you doing?"

"Oh, I'm doing fine. I'm making these Xs for my sins."

And my friend said, "So am I. I have to go back up to heaven to get my third piece of chalk!"

A Lucky Christmas

Robert R. Davila

John and Mary Noble lived in Vermont. Every day, John, who had worked as a fireman on a train before he retired, would get up and go out to the forest to chop wood. He would chop and chop away. Then he would bring the wood back home, stack some, and put the rest into the fireplace. His wife, Mary, used the fireplace to cook and warm the house. They had very little money, but they managed pretty well.

One morning, near Christmas 1945, John was taking his daily walk to the woods when he noticed a dog running beside him. It was a beautiful Irish setter. John knew that it was a hunting dog. He looked around to see whose dog it was, but there was no one around. He looked at the dog once more and then went into the forest.

John saw a good tree ahead of him, and he started hacking away at it. He noticed the dog was still circling around and around, looking at him and sniffing the ground. John left the dog alone and kept on chopping the tree. About half an hour later, he had chopped enough wood to last a few days. John only took home enough wood for one day. (He would go back and forth every day for as much as he needed.) He placed the wood in a sack, put it over his shoulder, and started to walk back home.

The dog started to follow John. John patted the dog on the head and kept walking toward his home. He forgot about the dog again. When John got home, he made a fire in the fireplace and put the rest of the wood away. After a while, it was time to wake up his wife. She got up, prepared breakfast, and they ate. Then John went outside.

The dog was sitting in the yard. John wondered to himself where in the world the owner could be. He called to Mary to come outside and see the dog. John explained that the dog had followed him into the forest and then followed him back home earlier that morning. He said that the dog was a most beautiful dog and Mary agreed. She, too, wondered where the owner might be. She said that the owner would probably come later to look for the dog.

All day and into the evening, the dog stayed in their yard. John and Mary thought that it was not right to keep the dog. So they opened the gate, let the dog out, and shut the gate behind it. They yelled to the dog to go away. Then they went to bed and slept through the night.

The next morning, John got up and dressed while his wife slept. He got his ax and started to go out to the forest to chop more wood. Just as he put the ax over his shoulder, he saw the dog in their yard again! John said to himself, "Boy, I love that dog and I also love to go hunting. Maybe he's a good hunting dog." So John went back into the house very quietly, put the ax back, and got his rifle.

He left the house with the dog. They went out, way out, into the forest, and they stayed all morning long. That dog was a wonderful dog indeed! He could point and do all the things a hunting dog was supposed to do. John shot birds and the dog caught a lot of them. He followed John all over the forest.

When John arrived home, he didn't know how to explain this to Mary. But he had to try. When he woke her up, she said, "What is it?" She sat up and looked around the room. "Look at all the beautiful birds you caught. How did you get them?" John explained that very early that morning he decided to go hunting with the dog instead of chopping wood. "I found out that the dog is a wonderful hunter, a great help to me."

After a while, Mary noticed that John was taking the dog with him—encouraging the dog to follow him. She didn't feel that was right. One day when John came home for lunch, Mary came to him and said, "Come here, I want to discuss something with you. I don't think it's right to keep that dog. It's not our dog. You had better go to town and knock on each door until you find the dog's owner. We should give it back." John thought that maybe Mary was right, so he said, "Okay. I will go to town."

That afternoon, John went to town. He knocked on doors but nobody knew anything about the dog. He went back home and said to Mary, "There is no owner."

She replied, "Well, I think it would be a good idea to put an ad in the newspaper. Perhaps someone will look in the newspaper and see that a dog has been found. Maybe someone's heart is broken. Or maybe children are crying over their missing dog. It's better to be honest about the whole thing and put the ad in the newspaper."

The next morning, John went to the newspaper office and explained that he wanted to put an ad in the newspaper. He found that it was cheaper to run the ad for seven days. So John put the ad in the newspaper for seven days. That evening, John opened up the newspaper and sure enough, there was his ad. After John finished reading the newspaper, he wanted to go hunting with the dog—he had gotten so attached to that dog, and he worried about that.

It was getting very close to Christmas. People were very busy shopping. John and Mary had been working hard to get ready. Everything was prepared for their holiday celebration. But still there was no answer to John's ad in the newspaper. No one came to claim the dog. Maybe someone had moved, or had lost the dog, or didn't even care about it. If seven days passed, John would be able to keep the dog.

On the seventh day of the ad, John felt anxious all day. He was working on the fence when he noticed a car on the road. This was unusual because there weren't many cars after the war. John saw that the car had pulled into his driveway. He started to feel quite depressed.

The young man who was driving the car must have been less than twenty-five years old. When he got out of the car, John and Mary could see that he was dressed very nicely. It looked as if the young man was quite well-to-do. He went up to John and said, "Excuse me, are you Mr. Noble who advertised in the paper for the lost dog?" John said, "Yes, I am."

The young man introduced himself, "My name is John Smith. I had a good hunting dog once, but I lost it. I thought perhaps you might have found my dog. May I see it?"

John looked around to see where the dog might be. He saw the dog a good distance away and yelled to it. The dog ran over to where they were standing and started walking around their feet. John said, "Is this your dog?"

The young man said, "I'm not sure, let me see. The dog has the same coloring as my dog—it looks very much the same. The dog has the same white dot on its forehead—looks almost identical. It's very hard to tell."

John said, "Well, what's your dog's name?"

"Henry."

"Well," John said, "let's call out Henry and see if the dog responds."

So the young man called out Henry, but the dog just looked up and looked back down on the ground and walked around. He called Henry again, and the dog didn't respond. Then John said, "The dog doesn't seem to be answering you."

The young man said, "Well, I guess it's not my dog. It doesn't answer to its name. My dog would answer that name immediately and look up."

John said that he was sorry. "Do you live around this area?"

The young man said yes. The young man then asked John if he had a dog. He also asked John if he ever went hunting.

"No, I don't have a dog, but yes, I have been hunting. Just a couple of days ago the dog and I went out hunting. This dog is a wonderful hunting dog. I really enjoy hunting with that dog, but I have to find its owner."

"That's not my dog," the young man said. "I'm sorry, I made a mistake. I thought maybe it was mine." John was quite relieved. He was glad that it wasn't the young man's dog. Now, he could keep it.

When the young man started to leave, John reached out to shake his hand. The man explained that he couldn't use his right hand anymore, but he shook hands with John using his left hand. John pitied the man; he had been hurt in the war. The young man got into his car and left. John ran into the house and told Mary what had happened. "It wasn't his dog. Maybe it will be ours; maybe we can keep it."

Mary said, "No, it's not ours. It's close to Christmas and someone might be heartbroken by the loss of that dog. We will have to wait one or two more days to be sure." John's hopes started to build again.

On December 24th, the day before Christmas, John got up to go hunting with the dog. They returned with several birds. While John and Mary were talking in the yard, they saw a Western Union bicycle coming. Before and during the war, people became nervous when they saw a Western Union bicycle coming. They knew it was bringing bad news. The news would hurt; a soldier had been wounded or had died. Now the war was over, but the telegram might still have bad news for someone.

The Western Union delivery boy came up to the house. John was scared to death. John knew the boy's name was Jimmy. John had seen him often. John said hello to Jimmy. "What are you doing here?" John asked.

Jimmy replied, "Hi there, Mr. Noble. I have a telegram for you."

"For me? I don't understand. Thank you, Jimmy."

Jimmy got on his bike and left. John went into the house. John was afraid to read the telegram. So was Mary. They opened the telegram and read it together. They were surprised by the message. "Try to call it Lucky." The telegram was signed, "A Friend." Mary said, "Oh, it must mean the dog." They ran outside to try the name.

The dog was standing a little ways off. John yelled out, "Lucky, Lucky!" The dog perked up its ears, ran towards John and jumped up on him. The dog licked John across the face. John had to push him down. It was the right name!

John thought about the telegram—how were the dog and the telegram related? Then John thought about the young man who had come yesterday—his right arm had been hurt in the war; he couldn't hunt anymore. Maybe that was why he didn't take the dog. John understood then.

The Ideal Preacher

Henry Holter

My story begins with a young college graduate who became a preacher. He was a very good speaker. He got a job in a town where the church was not very big. This preacher always preached about positive things. He never talked about negative things like sin, trouble, and fire, and all those things.

The church members liked the preacher very much—he made them happy and made them feel they were loved by God. They also liked him because he always limited his sermons to twenty minutes—never more, never less. He would stop right on the button, just twenty minutes. The entire service lasted one hour, which made the people quite happy. They never were bored.

One day a friend asked the preacher how he managed to meet that twenty-minute mark every Sunday. "That's simple," he answered. "Before I start preaching I always take out a Life Saver and put it in my mouth. When the Life Saver is gone, I know my time is up."

The preacher's reputation spread and the congregation grew. Many people came to hear this man preach. He made them so happy they gladly gave to the collection plate. They always went home happy. Now, if he had preached about hell and the devil and those things, they would not have liked it. They would not have been happy to give.

Church attendance grew quite substantially. The church became quite crowded. The wife who had always complained to her husband about sitting so close, had to learn to sit closer. This couple grew to love each other more; they learned to love each other all over again. Even though the church got more and more crowded (the church windows looked like eyes popping out), it did not collect much money. The preacher could not afford fine suits, so he went to the store and bought a humble, medium-priced suit. His wife thought that three buttons on the jacket cuff made the suit look ordinary, but four buttons would make it look like an expensive suit. So, she added one more button to each cuff.

One Sunday while the preacher was delivering his sermon, one of the buttons fell off. It dangled by a thread, so he quickly grabbed it and stashed it in his coat pocket. A few Sundays later, he was preaching away again. He had his Life Saver in his mouth, as usual, and he was sucking on it. But this Sunday the preacher talked for more than twenty minutes. He kept sucking his Life Saver and preaching. His wife noticed that the twenty minutes had passed, so she signaled to her husband that his time was up. The preacher was confused because he still had the Life Saver in his mouth, but he stopped preaching. After he sat down he took the Life Saver out of his mouth and got a big surprise. He had been sucking on the button the whole time!

The World's Largest Picture

Carl N. Schroeder

A long time ago there was a small village in the countryside. A river ran next to the village. The adults in the village worked out in the fields, tending to their crops and taking care of their farms. The children loved to sit and listen to an old man (the village storyteller) tell stories about many different things. Their favorite story was about the bridge that had been built many years ago by their forefathers. That bridge was very helpful to the village because it had opened up communication with the rest of the world. It was a very important bridge, and the people were very proud of it.

One day, a little boy asked the old man where the world's largest picture was. The old man thought and thought, but he did not know the answer.

"That's a good question," he said. "Where is the world's largest picture? Seems I'm going to have to travel to find out where the world's largest picture is. I'm going on a search. I'm going to cross the bridge and go out into the world to find the world's largest picture."

The old man left the village and started traveling over mountains and deserts and valleys, all over the country. He went to many different towns and asked many people where they thought the world's largest picture was. Some people said it was in the church and other people said it was in different places. It was very hard to find the exact location of the world's largest picture. So the old man continued his travels. On his way back home he met a salesman. The salesman had done quite a lot of traveling. The two men began to discuss their experiences. The old man told the salesman about his search for the world's largest picture. The salesman said he knew a little bit about that sort of thing. The old man listened and learned until, finally, he was ready to go back to the village.

The old man knew the people would be excited when he came back. He thought they would decorate the bridge and cheer when he came over it. After all, he was bringing news of the world's largest picture. When the old man came back, the village had a celebration. All the people were ready to listen, so the man told his story. He described the trees and the clouds and the birds and the sun and everything he had seen. Finally, somebody asked, "But where is the world's largest picture?" The old man answered, "It's right in your mind."

CHAPTER 12

My Summer Experience

Heimo I. Antila

In 1933, while I was a student at Gallaudet College, two friends and I decided to work as dishwashers during the summer. Pop Nelson, George Brown, and I got jobs at the Hotel Warren in Spring Lake, New Jersey. One day near the end of the summer, Pop asked me if I could drive him to Asbury Park, New Jersey, so he could buy a pair of shoes. I said I was sorry, but I could not do it. He then turned to George and asked him to drive to Asbury Park. I asked George if he had a license. He said no, he was from Ohio where a license was not necessary. I was very naive and let him drive my car to Asbury Park. Two hours later George and Pop returned frowning and looking very glum.

"What's wrong? What happened?"

George Brown said, "Well, I drove your car through the train crossing barrier, and the barrier broke; and the train barrier smashed in the windshield of your car."

I regretted letting them take the car. Then I wondered about the police. "Did anybody copy down the tag number of my car?"

George said yes.

I knew if I stayed in the state I would be liable for a $50 fine for letting someone without a license use my car. I approached the hotel steward and said, "I want to quit today. I have to go home; I received some bad news. I want my pay now."

The steward started hassling with me. "No, you have to stay here. You have to stay until after Labor Day. We'll have great crowds of people coming. It will be hard for two people to do the work. We need all three dishwashers."

"No, I must leave now," I replied.

We argued for a while. Then an hour later he paid me. I took my money, packed my things, and drove off with the wind blowing in my face.

I didn't feel comfortable at all because of the wind. I noticed a junkyard on the side of the road, so I pulled over and stopped. I went in and got the owner. I told him I wanted to see if he had a car like mine there—I wanted to buy the windshield from it. I asked how much it would cost, and he said $5. He told me to look for it myself. It was dark, so I used a flashlight to locate one. I found one, so I removed the windshield and put it in my car. After that I waved goodbye and drove to New York City.

This was my first time driving in New York City in the middle of the night. When I noticed a red light several blocks away, I drove across several intersections until I got to the intersection where the red light was and then I stopped. I repeated this maneuver three or four times until a police officer caught up with me and cut me off. When the police officer started speaking to me, I motioned to him that I was deaf. He pulled out a pad of paper and started writing. Then, he handed me the pad.

"When you see the red light way down there, five blocks ahead, you have to stop at the very next block. And do that every time you see it—stop at the next block. You gave everyone a bad scare. Some cars had to dart around you. You could have caused a tremendous accident on the street. Can you read English?"

I answered, "Oh, yes I can. Are you going to give me a ticket?"

"No!"

"Thanks."

I put the note in my pocket and drove out of New York City. On the highway I got stuck behind a garbage truck that smelled terrible. The truck had Connecticut tags. I waited for a chance to pass the truck. When I did, it passed me. I passed it again . . . it passed me again, too. I slowed up to put some distance between us, but the truck also slowed up. The driver must have wanted me to enjoy the smell—all the way to Bridgeport, Connecticut!

I arrived home in Massachusetts all right. When I returned to Gallaudet in the fall, I found a letter waiting for me from the New Jersey Central Railroad. I opened it up; it was a fine for breaking the train barrier—$16. Sixteen dollars? I didn't know where I was going to get $16. Then, I figured it out—George Brown had driven the car and hadn't watched where he was going, so he could pay $5, Pop Nelson had asked George to drive him so he could buy those shoes, so he could pay $5. And I was stupid enough to let them both go and do it, so I decided to go ahead and pay the balance of $6 to punish myself.

My First Deaf Model

Lynn Jacobowitz

L et me tell you a bit about my background. I went to elementary and secondary oral schools. All of my teachers were oralists. I would read their lips and interpret to my classmates on the sly. I did not have my first deaf teacher until I came to Gallaudet College. Her name was Judy Williams. She taught English.

The first day of classes I came into the classroom and sat down. The teacher walked in and started signing in ASL. I looked at one of my classmates and asked him if the teachers here signed. He said yes. The other students all nodded and said signs were allowed at Gallaudet. I didn't feel very comfortable with this; I still resisted sign language.

The teacher asked us to write compositions. We all wrote short paragraphs, and the teacher taped them on the wall. We looked at each others' compositions; it was very interesting. The teacher than looked at them. The first one got an F. The next one got a D. Then an F, D, F, as she continued down the wall. We were all very depressed. This deaf teacher was really mean. I thought she didn't know anything about English. We started arguing among ourselves.

The teacher slammed her fist on the desk and told us to pay attention, to look at her. But I was still very resistant. She was signing, but I wasn't comfortable with that. She explained why the errors were there and I was very fascinated with her explanation. I was drawn to her, I felt she was my friend, yet I resisted for a long time.

About a month later, I started to believe that she really was a good teacher. She increased my confidence in writing. Not only in writing compositions, but in writing plays and poetry, too. I wrote and wrote until I was deranged with writing. If it hadn't been for the fact that she was a deaf teacher maybe my writing would have gotten worse. I think it really pays to have deaf teachers for all subjects.

I learned a lot from Judy Williams in a short time. She showed me it was important to have deaf teachers. She had a great influence on me. Sadly, she died in a freak car accident. I was quite depressed when I learned that news. But she will always be my first deaf model.

Some Funny Things Happened Along the Way

Thomas K. Holcomb

Since my graduation from Gallaudet College two years ago, I have worked as a student recruiter for Gallaudet. My primary responsibility is to visit different schools for the deaf in the United States and speak to the students—explain to them about Gallaudet and why they should attend Gallaudet. During my travels to different states, many funny things have happened to me because of my deafness. For example, when I get on a plane, I like to sit by the window so I can look out. I never bother to look around me on the plane. One time a woman tapped me on the shoulder and started speaking, but I didn't understand her. So, I wrote her a note to ask her what she was trying to say. She said she was trying to make conversation with me, but she thought I was a snob. Then I told her I was deaf and said I was sorry, and we both began talking. Looking back, I wonder how many people have tried to make conversation with me before. I guess I'll never know.

Often when I travel on planes in the morning, I try to order orange juice. I'll order it and invariably I'll get a Coke. No matter how we try to communicate—with lipreading, gestures, and all that—I still get a Coke. That's sad. Just because I can't speak well. Oh well.

One time I was traveling with another recruiter. We sat down in the airport to wait for the plane. We knew that the plane was very, very small, that it only had a few seats. We agreed that we would hurry on the plane and try to get two seats together. So, we waited near the hallway until we thought our plane was there. There was an announcement, so we ran down this long hallway to get onto the plane, but then we found out we were wrong; it was not our plane. We were embarrassed. All these people behind us were lined up and waiting. We had ha hard time getting through the crowd back to the lobby. It was really embarrassing. So the next time we had to wait, we made sure that we had the right plane before we got on it.

I had another interesting experience in California. I was supposed to visit a high school. On the morning of my visit, I got up, looked at my watch, and realized I was very late. I was all excited; I hurried to get my clothes on and get in my car and go. I even finished dressing in the car. As I was driving, it was dark and there was nobody on the road. I thought that was strange—there was no traffic at all. I made really good time. When I got to the school the fence was locked—it was closed and there were no cars inside. I looked at my watch; it was the right time for my appointment. As a matter of fact, I was a little bit late. And then all of a sudden I remembered the three-hour time difference between Washington, D.C. and California. I guess I was so tired I just forgot about the three-hour difference. So I drove back to my hotel, slept for a few more hours, and then got up, got ready, and arrived right on time. If I had been hearing maybe I could have asked a hotel clerk to call and wake me up on time. But I'm deaf.

One thing I've noticed about schools with mainstreaming programs is that they are very much the same. When I go into the office and ask for the deaf department they say, "Oh, it's down this hall and around this way." Then they say they would be very happy to take me to this particular room. And always it's down this way and around the corner and all the way to the end of the building. At every school it's the same thing. I wonder why the deaf people are always put in the back and not in the front of the building. I have no idea. But it is an interesting observation—these programs are all the same.

So you can see that many, many frustrating things happen to me, but they really make my job more interesting and more enjoyable. All in all, recruiting has been a wonderful experience.

An Itchy Story

Heimo I. Antila

During my sophomore year in college, my fraternity (Kappa Gamma) planned a dance. While we were working in the Ole Jim, decorating the place, I felt that we ought to have some garland greenery hanging from the rafters. We discussed it and wondered where we could find garlands. "Oh," I said, "there's some in the woods on the Gallaudet campus, behind the farm." So we all got together and walked to the woods.

The first tree we came to was a great, big, tall one with a green vine growing up it. I saw three leaves in clusters all around and I knew that it was poison ivy. I tried to dissuade my fraternity brothers from picking it. I told them that it was poison ivy. And the guys (they were upperclassmen) said, "Oh, you're stupid. That's Virginia Creeper."

"Virginia Creeper? But my father told me that a three-leaf configuration is poison ivy."

We started fussing at each other, and then I dropped the argument. I said I would help them. We pulled down the vines from that tree and carried them into the Ole Jim. We started decorating. After a while, Professor Drake showed up. He was curious to see what we all were doing in the Ole Jim. He looked at everything and said, "I'm a farmer. I know that's poison ivy you are handling. I teach agriculture here at the college."

We looked at him and said, "Oh, you're in agriculture. Better call in Professor Allison who teaches botany. Maybe he knows more."

Professor Allison came in and saw the poison ivy. He said, "I'm surprised at all of you, you are ignorant! Don't you know that a vine with three leaves is always poison ivy? Virginia Creeper has clusters of five leaves."

I knew he was right; so I suggested we take all the poison ivy back to the woods. We put it over our shoulders again and carried it back to the woods. Well that evening at the Kappa Gamma dance, I noticed some of my fraternity brothers were missing. What happened to them? I found out they were in their rooms in College Hall, in bed, all swollen, itchy, red, and scratching themselves.

The poison ivy had no effect on me. When I was a prep, I had applied iodine to an abrasion on my elbow, which made it swell and look like poison ivy. The doctor had given me an injection that made me immune to poison ivy. What I am allergic to is iodine!

My Life on Kendall Green

Agnes Padden

I always tell people that Kendall Green is my second home because I've lived or worked here almost all my life. I think I am the only person who has watched Kendall Green change over the years because I've never moved out of the Washington, D.C. area. I attended Kendall School and then I entered Gallaudet College as a preparatory student. I really had many happy years on this campus, especially at Kendall School and Gallaudet College. After I graduated from Gallaudet, I became a teacher and taught preschool at Kendall School. Then I worked at the Tutorial Center and later I transferred to the English Department, where I have been teaching for the past sixteen years.

I remember when Kendall Green was "country" in the city. Everything was green, there were trees all around. The Kendall girls and I would take walks to the farm that was on one side of the campus. When I was in Kendall School, I lived in a dormitory on the campus. The dorm was House #4 (which is now the Office of Demographic Studies); it used to have a porch with a rail in front of it. On spring evenings after supper, we girls were allowed to go out and play for a while. We played on the half of the campus in front of the dorm—we rode our bicycles and roller-skated all the way up to the Ole Jim and then we turned around and came back to House #1 (the President's House).

While we were out playing, the college girls and boys would be out walking past our dorm. The college girls could go outside after supper for Campus Hour. The college students walked in pairs all over the campus. When we saw the couples coming we all stopped playing, sat on the porch rail, and watched the couples walking by. These couples always stopped talking because they didn't want us to watch their conversations. They walked past us looking straight ahead. Once, our supervisor told us that we should not do this because the college girls said we all looked like chickens on the rail staring at them.

During the winter the Kendall girls and I often saw the college boys playing near College Hall. One winter evening when there was deep snow, we saw the boys running back and forth, stark naked, in front of College Hall. So you see, there were streakers in the 1940s, which shows that streaking was not something new in the 1970s.

My college years were wonderful years. We had good teachers. I can recall vividly two of my teachers because they really influenced me. Dr. Elizabeth Peet, who was Dean of Women at that time, was a very refined woman. She was well mannered and dignified, and she tried to make ladies of all of us. Frederick Hughes was the other teacher whom I remember vividly. All the students loved him. He taught classes in dramatics and current events.

During my senior year I decided to participate in a musical play that Professor Hughes was directing—*The Mikado*. I had a leading role in *The Mikado*. The play took place in Japan. Now, there was one scene in which my lover and I had to kiss each other. Professor Hughes didn't want us to do that in public because he was worried about what people in the audience would say. He knew Dr. Peet would be in the audience. He thought about how we could change that scene. For the play I wore a kimono and a black wig, so Professor Hughes decided to give me a Japanese fan. My lover and I practiced bowing our heads together behind the fan to make it look as if we were actually kissing. We practiced over and over again.

On opening night, as we were doing this scene, I opened up the fan and my lover and I bowed our heads down behind the fan. Guess what happened? My lover kissed me so hard that I was stunned for a few minutes. I forgot my lines. I found out later that Professor Hughes was so surprised to see us actually kissing that he became flabbergasted and said, "No! No, no, don't do that." After that my lover decided to cooperate with Professor Hughes. He did not kiss me anymore.

There was another incident that I remember clearly. Several of my classmates and I were hungry one afternoon. It was 2:30 and we were not allowed to go off the campus until 4:00. We wanted to get something to eat, so we thought we would go across the street to a corner drugstore and order sandwiches or ice cream sodas. When a girl wanted to go off campus, she had to sign her name in a book in the dorm. We all wondered if we should sign the book or let Dr. Peet get mad at us. We decided that we would just walk off the campus and come right back. Just as we all filed out of Fowler Hall (our dormitory), we saw Dr. Peet waiting to get across the street. We all turned around, ran back into Fowler Hall, and hid in the basement. We waited and waited. After a while the girls told me to go upstairs to see if Dr. Peet would say anything. I went all the way up to the third floor so I could pretend that I was just coming down from there. As I was coming down the steps, I saw Dr. Peet looking at the book that didn't have our names in it. Dr. Peet said to one of the students, "I saw many young ladies leaving the campus and they all ran back to the dorm. Do you know who they were?" She never did find out who tried to sneak off that afternoon.

As I said before, Dr. Peet tried to make ladies of us. One afternoon I decided to chew gum while roaming in the hall. Dr. Peet came up to me and said, "Do you know it's not dignified for a young lady to chew gum in public? You look like a cow chewing its cud. Please go to your room and sit down and chew to your heart's content. Then, throw the gum in the wastebasket before you come out."

There are many, many other things that I remember. I feel that Dr. Peet and Professor Hughes made my life very exciting. They gave me many memories to look back on.

Douglas Craig, M.M.

Heimo I. Antila

I have a very interesting story about Douglas Craig, M.M. (That M.M. stood for Master of Mail.) Dr. Edward M. Gallaudet found Douglas Craig when he was a young boy wandering the streets of Washington, D.C. Gallaudet discovered that Craig was deaf, and so he brought him to Kendall Green. Craig worked as a handy man at the College until his death. His duty for many years was to carry the mail back and forth from Gallaudet College to the post office. Craig was a very powerful man. We never knew his age.

I entered the preparatory class at Gallaudet in 1929. All of the new students were called preps. One night some of the upperclassmen blindfolded us (the preps) and forced us all into a room, one at a time. When my turn came, they led me down the hall and made me stand against the wall. Then suddenly they pulled by blindfold down. I saw in front of me a fierce-looking black man with a knife in his hand. Several upperclassmen were trying to restrain him. The man threatened me and said, "Come here, give me some money."

I looked around and asked, "Who are you? What money? And, for what?"

The man said that he was Douglas Craig and that I owed him three dollars because he had carried my trunk up to the fourth floor. He said that I had to pay it immediately.

"Now? I must pay that money now? Okay, okay." I took three dollars out of my pocket and gave it to him.

When I left, Craig called for the next prep, and he repeated the same procedure. He did the same thing to all the preps. I felt sorry for all of us. We were scared to death.

The next day I got over the scare. From that point on, for months until springtime, I forgot all about it. Then one day the upperclassmen decided to call all the preps together. They told us that we all had to go camping in Great Falls, Virginia, with them. Many of us said that we had no money left. They started laughing and told us not to worry. They reminded us about last fall when Douglas Craig had threatened us with a knife to collect three dollars. We all had given him the money. Well, the upperclassmen had saved all that money and now they were giving it back to us for our camping fees.

Thanksgiving Tug-o-War

Donald A. Padden

Gallaudet College is rich in tradition. Many traditions that originated in the early years of Gallaudet College have become obsolete and have been replaced by new traditions. Few of the old traditions remain in existence today. One of my favorites was the Thanksgiving Tug-o-War.

Each year at Gallaudet, new students had to undergo a period of hazing. In order to distinguish them from older students, the new students had to wear buff and blue dink or beanie caps and red bandannas in their coat pockets from the opening of the academic year until Thanksgiving. On Thanksgiving Day they were challenged to a tug-o-war by the freshman students. If they succeeded in beating the freshmen two out of three times in the contest, they were free to discard the caps and bandannas. If they failed, they had to continue wearing the caps and bandannas until Christmas.

Several upperclassmen served on the Tug-o-War Committee. The committee's responsibility was to select an equal number of participants from the two classes. The two groups had to weigh the same amount. On Thanksgiving morning, which was usually cold and frosty, the two groups met on the Faculty Row lawn. After tying a red cloth at the middle point of the rope, the committee put the two groups on the opposite sides of the rope. To make the contest more exciting for the fans, the committee borrowed a hose from the neighboring fire department. They used it to spray cold water at the red cloth on the rope. When the committee chairperson gave the go signal, the two opposing groups grunted and groaned and tried to pull each other into the path of the water. The water was really cold. When a person of either group entered the area of cold water, he just lost his strength and became useless to his team. The team who had the most members in the water usually lost.

The upperclassmen really tried to make it difficult for the preps to win the match. If the preps won the first trial, the committee would declare a mistrial due to a foul and cancel it. That gave the freshmen another chance to win the match and save their reputation. However, if the preps still won two out of the next three trials, the committee had to award the victory to them. The committee had to release the preps from their cap and bandanna bondage. It is not surprising that over the years that freshman classes won the tug-o-war contests most of the time.

College Hall Revisited

Francis C. Higgins

Gerald Burstein was a student at Gallaudet College back in the 1950s. At that time it was against the rules to have a girl in College Hall because it was the men's dormitory. One day, Gerald's sister came to visit him in his room. In the middle of their visit, they heard a knock on the door. Gerald was frightened. He thought maybe it was a teacher who had come to check on him. He asked his sister to hide in the closet. The closet didn't have a door, only drapes. Gerald put his sister in the closet and closed the drapes. Then he went to the door, opened it, and saw an old man there.

The old man said, "I used to live in this room. I'd appreciate it if you would permit me to come in and look around my old room."

So Gerald invited him in. The old man looked around slowly and said, "Same old room." Then he walked to the window, looked out for a while, and turned around and said, "Same old view." Just as he was starting to walk away, he noticed a pair of women's shoes sticking out from under the drapes. He smiled and said, "Same old tricks."

Gerald became embarrassed and said, "I didn't mean to do anything wrong; she's my sister. We thought you were a faculty member, so I hid my sister in the closet."

The old man smiled again and said, "Same old alibi."

Do Deaf People Have Ears?

Francis C. Higgins

When Dr. Edward Miner Gallaudet was president of Gallaudet College, it was customary for the students to meet in Chapel Hall every Sunday evening to listen to his lectures. One night, President Gallaudet introduced a famous visitor to the students. He explained the visitor's background. After the introduction, the visitor stood up and looked over the student body. He had a look of surprise on his face. The visitor turned to Dr. Gallaudet and asked, "Are these people deaf?"

Dr. Gallaudet replied, "Yes, they're all deaf; they are students here at Gallaudet College."

The visitor said, "But these people have ears!"

CHAPTER 13

Why Hearing Miners Got up Late One Morning

Francis C. Higgins

Many, many years ago in a small town in Montana, one deaf man worked in a mine. The deaf man had a special way to wake himself up in the morning for work. He threw a rope over a pulley that hung from the ceiling and he tied one end to his alarm clock. When the clock rang, it disconnected the rope, and a heavy old-fashioned iron tied to the other end of the rope would fall onto the floor. Every time that iron fell on the floor it would make a loud noise, and that would wake up the deaf man. The noise also woke up all the other miners in the small town. They became accustomed to using that noise to wake themselves up.

One day the deaf miner got married. He and his wife went away for their honeymoon. Three days later, they returned. They were surprised to find the whole town so quiet. All of the miners were still sleeping because they hadn't yet heard the iron fall.

A Ghost Story

Cheryl Shevlin

A deaf couple in Texas wanted to buy a house. They walked around town looking for one to buy. They saw a beautiful house and they looked it over. They both really liked the house, so they wrote down the address and then asked one of their mothers to make a telephone call to the real estate agent. The real estate agent met them at the house. They knocked on the door and met the owner, an older man who seemed to be peevish. After a while, the real estate agent left.

The man and woman went into the house. She thought it was a beautiful house. They walked to the kitchen, which was huge, and then to the living room, which was also huge. The fireplace was very nice, and all the rooms had high ceilings. They were curious about the upstairs, so they walked up the steps. There was a black cat sitting on the landing. It didn't move, it just sat there. The couple looked around the bedrooms—even those rooms were huge. The bathroom was very long and large. The couple really liked that house. The owner told them to make an offer, so they put down a deposit. Then, they went home and discussed whether they should buy the house. They decided they could afford it. They met with the owner and bought it.

Soon, the husband and wife packed and moved into their beautiful house. It didn't need a lot of improvement or work in the backyard. They bought furniture to furnish the house. After a few weeks, they were settled in and enjoying their new house. One night as they were in bed, talking with each other, they noticed the wind outside was blowing up a storm. They felt the house bouncing and rumbling. They grabbed hold of each other until the rumbling stopped.

A few weeks later they felt the rumbling and the noise again. That awful vibration! The cat jumped up on the window sill; they were really scared. They looked outside; they knew it was the time of year that Texas tended to have a lot of wind and storms. A month or so later, it happened again. They could feel a vibration along the floor. It was really frightening. The noise was very odd. They got up and turned on the lights and then felt the wall. It was strange—this wall had become so thin in a certain place that there was an indentation. There was a closet. It was never used. There was tape around the door knob and across the keyhole. The husband and wife thought that was really odd. They didn't remember this closet.

They went back to bed. A little bit later the rumbling and the vibrations started again. They didn't understand what was happening. They went over to the wall and felt it. Yes, it was the wall that was vibrating. They looked at each other and at the door, trying to decide whether they should open it. Just then, the black cat jumped up on the window sill. That did it, they decided not to open the door.

The next morning they called the wife's mother. They asked her to come over and listen to the wall and find out what the noise was. She told them they had very active imaginations. They agreed, but told her the next time they felt that vibration, they would call her. So they waited, until finally the wind howled and the vibration started. They called the mother and she came over. She said she could feel the vibration and hear that strange noise. Then, she felt along the wall. She went downstairs to get a hammer to break open the door. When she got the door open, they were shocked. They could see a skeleton hanging there, bouncing against the wall. A skeleton!

Oops!

Francis C. Higgins

S ome years ago, a group of teachers at a school for the deaf were sitting in a room, waiting for the teachers' meeting to begin. A few hearing teachers were sitting together and talking. A deaf teacher was sitting in a corner of the room. After a while, the deaf teacher got up, walked over to the hearing teachers, and asked what they were talking about. One signed to the deaf teacher that they were talking about the Lindbergh kidnapping trial. "What do think about that?" The deaf person thought and said, "Oh, excuse me," and went back to his chair. After a while, he got up and walked back to the hearing teachers and said, "I've been thinking a lot about this. I'm sure there was more than one man involved." The hearing teachers laughed hard about that. The deaf teacher became embarrassed and asked what was wrong. One of them signed to him, "We are talking about the Dionne quintuplets now."

Poor Beethoven

Francis C. Higgins

O ne night, several years ago, two pianists were playing in a hotel in Washington, D.C. When they finished playing the *Moonlight Sonata*, an elderly woman came over and gave them some compliments. She told the two men that they were wonderful pianists and that she really enjoyed their music. She wanted to know who had written that sonata. One of the pianists responded and told her that Beethoven had written it many years ago. He also added it was really wonderful how Beethoven could write many, many different kinds of music, even though he was deaf. The elderly woman said, "What? Deaf—oh I am so sorry." Then she turned and walked away.

Several days later, the two pianists received a package with a letter attached. They opened the package and found a hearing aid. When they read the letter, they discovered that it was from the elderly woman. In the letter she asked them to give the hearing aid to poor Beethoven!

Candy or Death

Robert G. Sanderson

I would like to tell you a true story based on my past experience as a rehabilitation counselor. One day a young man came in to see me. His name was Bill. He sat down and we looked at each other. I really felt sorry for him. He had bumps all over his face—awful red and yellow bumps, pimples and blisters. And that young man didn't feel well either—he felt dizzy and sick.

Bill and I talked for a while, and I decided I could help him. I explained to him that the rehabilitation program required several things before I could help. First, I had to send him to a doctor for an examination to make sure he was healthy and to test his nose, mouth, and ears—to see if he was really deaf or not. If he was deaf then I could help him. Bill seemed to understand all this, so I went ahead and sent him to the doctor for a physical.

A week or two later Bill came back again. I had received the doctor's report, which was very bad. That young man had diabetes, and he needed shots of insulin. I explained to Bill that he must learn how to inject insulin.

Bill said, "You mean shoot needles into myself?!"

I said, "Oh, it's nothing; you can do it. It's easy."

"But I've never done that," he said. "I can't do it, I'm so frightened. Put needles in my arm? No. I'm too scared."

So I said, "The doctor explained to you that you're sick."

"Oh, I didn't understand. He kept talking, but I couldn't read his lips. And when he wrote things down, I couldn't understand it."

I brought out the doctor's report. "The doctor says that you have sugar diabetes very badly. If you eat candy, you could become very sick. You could go into shock and you could die!"

Bill looked at me and said, "Die? I eat candy all the time and I haven't died."

I said, "Maybe not now, but later on if you eat too much candy, it would really hit you and you would faint. If people didn't know what was wrong and just left you there, you would die."

Bill looked at me and said, "Really? Really?"

"Yes."

"Oh, I'm easily tempted. I just love candy!"

I said, "Well you must make a choice—your health or your death. You can prevent that death with the insulin. The doctor will show you how to take the medicine; you fill up the needle and inject it in your arm."

Bill was frightened. I said, "Well, it's your choice. I want to help you, but you must cooperate."

"What am I going to do?"

I said, "I'll buy the needle for you and I will get the medicine for you, give you help, show you how to use it, and everything. I will help you do it. You must do it, okay?"

Bill was still worried. "I don't want to use a needle," he said.
"It's your responsibility. I told you I can't help you if you don't cooperate. Rehabilitation means help. If you die I can't help you. I can't send you to school. I can't get you training for a job if you don't cooperate with me. But if you take the medicine every day, you will be better. Your face is so bad now. Doesn't it bother you when you look in the mirror every morning? You know that it's from the diabetes, from too much sugar. Do you want to look good? Do you want the girls to look at you and like you? Now girls look at you and think your face looks awful and they stay away from you. Am I right, am I right?"

"Yes."

I said, "Well, okay!" Later on I bought the needle. I went ahead and bought the medicine, too, and called Bill to come back again. I gave everything to him. I explained how to use it, all the different steps, and he promised he would use it.

A week passed, then two weeks went by—I was waiting to hear from Bill. I hadn't seen him again and I was wondering if something had happened to him. I went to look for him and found him in his apartment. He was so sick, he couldn't see me.

I said, "Did you finish using that medicine?"

He said, "No I haven't, yet. I'm afraid."

Well, being a counselor I had to help this individual, but how? He was stubborn and afraid. I explained to him, "If you're afraid to take the shots yourself, you'll have to go to the doctor regularly, every morning at the same time. The doctor will give you the shots."

He said, "I don't have the time!"

I said, "The time! Then do it yourself; it would be easy—you could give yourself the insulin shot and go to work. Do you want to go to the doctor every morning and waste your time?"

He said, "No."

"Well now, I want to help you, so I'll show you how to boil the needle. You boil it in hot water, take it out, fill it up with insulin, and you put it in your arm."

I showed him how and I let him try it for the first time. He made a mistake, he tried again, and he fainted. Fainted flat on the floor. So, I waited. As soon as he felt better I showed him how to do it again. Still he wouldn't. Then, I noticed his wastebasket—it was full of crumpled candy wrappers. He loved candy! I said "You better stop eating candy. That would help you."

He said, "I like it, I love candy."

"Okay, I warned you. I have to leave now, but I'll see you later. You come to my office and we'll talk more. I'll explain to you some other things. Now don't you eat candy or you will be sick. Don't eat that candy. Come and see me tomorrow."

"Okay."

Bill came to see me the next day. I planned a little bit of a surprise for that boy. That morning I went to a mortuary (a funeral home) and asked the funeral director if he would loan me his book of pictures of coffins. I explained to him why and he lent me the book. I brought it to my office. When Bill came in, I said, "Bill, I have something for you." He looked at me with a puzzled expression.

I said, "I'll show you." I opened up the book, pointed and said, "These are coffins. I would like for you to pick a beautiful one for yourself. One you would like to be buried in."

He was so afraid! He said "No! No!"

I said "Yes! Bill, pick the one that you want. Not many people have an opportunity to pick their own coffins. Now you have a chance to look at all the different coffins—before you die! That's wonderful!"

Bill said, "No, no, no, no!" His face was white.

"What are you afraid of? What's the matter? You can get a nice, soft, white, satin one. Or, maybe you like the red or pink better. You can lay on something comfortable. You can feel how comfortable before you die!"

"No, no, no!" He pushed the book away and closed it. "I don't want that, I don't want that, I don't want that!"

I said, "Bill, you're going to die soon because your diabetes is very bad. I've tried to help you. If you want to go ahead and keep eating candy, you must be prepared to die. So, pick your coffin now!"

Bill said, "No, no, no!"

He would say nothing but that—No, no! So, I pushed the book aside. Bill sat with his eyes closed—he was shocked. After a while he looked up at me. "Do you really mean this?"

"Yes, I mean this. I'm not teasing you!"

"Yes, I see."

"You must have the shots!"

"Yes, you're right, I must. Okay."

So, I helped Bill from there on in. Well, a few years passed by. One day Bill came to see me again. His face was clean; all those bumps were gone. Bill looked pretty good!

"How are you?"

He said, "Dr. Sanderson, now I have a girlfriend."

"Fine, a girlfriend! Plan to get married someday?"

"Oh yes!"

"That's wonderful. Bill, are you eating candy still?"

"No!"

And that's the end of my story.

The First Deaf Postmaster

Hubert Anderson, Jr.

I think it is important to share experiences with others, so I would like to tell a story about my life. Many years ago I went out in search of a job. One day I had an interview with a man at American University in Washington, D.C. This man told me that he would consider hiring me as a postal clerk and that he would be in touch with me later. I thanked him and left. A few days later the interviewer called and asked me to come back. I went in early the next morning. The interviewer told me that he had decided to give me the job. I was very happy about becoming a postal clerk.

During my first few months I got to know my co-workers, who were all hearing people. I taught them sign language and they taught me about postal work. I learned a lot from them. I was very motivated and I made many friends. American University had a very large post office system. But communication was a problem in the beginning. Later on, almost all of my co-worker became skilled in sign language.

During my fourth year at American University, my boss was promoted to another job. It was necessary for him to select someone to take over the job of postmaster. I happened to be in a very good position for getting that job because of my experience and because I was a good worker; there was no comparison between me and the others. But I happened to be deaf. I had to have an interview for the new job. In the interview my boss asked me if I thought my deafness would be a problem. I told him no, that many other deaf people in the United States had been promoted in their jobs. The important thing was to be given the chance.

My boss wasn't worried about my skills, he was worried about the other people. In the end, he decided to give me the position. He announced his decision to all of the postal workers. A few of the workers said, "But, he's deaf, he can't control us."

I was really surprised that my co-workers would insult me like that. In the past we had been friends, good friends; I had taught them sign language and we had shared stories about our lives. But on the day the boss picked me to become postmaster, a few of them were really upset. They said I couldn't handle the job. They were very negative. But the boss had made his decision and he stuck by it.

On my first day as postmaster I tried my best to make the workers (there were about 60 of them) understand that I would be flexible and fair. Work continued day after day, and most of the time things went smoothly. However, in my first year I had to fire eleven of my workers. They never gave me their full cooperation. Sometimes, they wouldn't even give me phone messages.

Very often when a deaf person takes over or becomes the boss, some of the hearing workers object. They may not be used to working with a deaf person, or they may not really understand deafness. But if the deaf person does a good job and is fair, then there won't be any problems. I worked as postmaster for five years. My workers recognized that a deaf person could do a good job.

One day a deaf man from Gallaudet College came over to American University to visit me and see my post office. He was very surprised to see a deaf person in control of that big post office, especially with all of those hearing people working under me. I showed him around my post office. He asked me if I would be interested in transferring to Gallaudet College's post office. I told him maybe because there was no place for me to advance at American University. So, he went back to Gallaudet College to arrange a way for me to transfer.

A few weeks later I received a letter asking me to come to Gallaudet College for an interview. I remember that interview very well; there were about fifteen people seated around asking me questions. Many of the questions were very easy for me to answer because of my experience in a large post office. Gallaudet had a small post office, so it would be easy for me to manage it.

The next day the secretary called me to offer me the job at Gallaudet, and I accepted. Even though Gallaudet had a small post office, I really enjoyed my job—no more of the headaches I had in the big post office.

I want young deaf people to know that they can be successful at something, if they try! Don't think negatively about deafness; think positively about achieving success.

CHAPTER 14

An Embarrassing Moment

Leon Auerbach

I n 1943, during the war years, I was working and living in Cambridge, Massachusetts. My wife and I lived on the third floor of an apartment building. One night we took a trolley to visit some friends outside of Boston. We played cards and talked and talked late into the night—it was past one o'clock in the morning when we left. It was so late we got the last trolley back to Cambridge. We arrived home and walked up to the third floor of our building. It was then I realized that I had forgotten my keys—I had left them inside my apartment. I was afraid it was not going to be easy to get into the apartment. My wife and I decided to go look for the watchman, but the watchman was off at that late hour; he had already gone home.

My wife and I began to wonder how in the world we were going to get into our apartment. I said to my wife, "The police station must have some kind of pass or master key. They could get us in."

So, I decided to walk to the police station. I wrote a note explaining that my wife and I were locked out of our apartment because I had forgotten my keys. I told the police we had been visiting friends outside of Boston. The police officer asked why we didn't go back to our friends' apartment. I said we couldn't; all of the trolleys had stopped for the night. There was just no way to get there. The police sergeant said he had to go talk with another police officer. Then the other police officer came back and put on his coat and his hat. I asked him what was going on. He told me to go with him.

The police officer and I walked out and got into his car. We rode over to the firehouse. I suddenly thought to myself, the firehouse would have the pass key, it was the logical place, not the police station. Why should the police station have the key? I should have gone to the firehouse in the first place.

When we got to the firehouse, the police officer told me to wait while he went inside. I waited outside. I thought he would be getting the keys. All of a sudden, the big doors opened up and the hook and ladder truck (you know the truck with two drivers; one in the back, one in the front) came out. The firefighters had on their full gear. I thought to myself, "Oh, my gosh, there must be a big fire somewhere around here."

We got back into the car, and the police officer said, "Let's go, you show us the way." I gave him directions to my apartment. All of a sudden, the hook and ladder started flashing its lights and following us! Boy, I was so embarrassed. When we arrived at the apartment house, the fire truck unhooked the ladder and raised it up to the third floor. By this time all the neighbors were poking their heads out their windows to see what was going on. One of the firefighters climbed up the ladder and crawled through one of our windows. Then he opened our door from the inside and welcomed us in. All I could say was thank you very much. I never felt so embarrassed.

A Close Brush with Death

Frances M. Parsons

Part One

When I was twelve years old, my family moved to Tahiti. We took a boat across the Pacific Ocean. Tahiti is a very small island located between South America and Australia. My family lived there for six years—the first four years were very happy ones. It was paradise. We could swim, canoe, horseback ride—do just about anything. And then World War II broke out. Because Tahiti was controlled by France and France was at war with Germany, we felt the impact of war.

You can imagine how much food the French soldiers needed. French ships would land on the island, and the soldiers would go to the Chinese merchants and take their flour for bread. The Chinese merchants were not happy about turning over their flour to the French soldiers. Not at all! They hid their flour for their own businesses. This, however, was not such a good idea because Tahiti is very hot and humid. Bugs and maggots grew in the hidden flour sacks. Whenever we made bread, we had to take out the bugs and maggots before we could eat it!

Conditions got worse and worse during the war. Some big ships came and took away many of the Americans who were worried and in a hurry to return to America. My family also wanted to leave Tahiti. We lived forty-five miles from Papeete, the capital city. We packed our things and then drove four hours in a truck to Papeete. On the way, we had to stop to pick up some pigs and chickens for our trip. When we arrived, the boat was already filled with passengers. We felt very frustrated. We had waited one-and-a-half years and we couldn't seem to get out. The situation got worse and worse. There was no food, no paper, no supplies, and no canned goods. We really suffered.

A French captain, who was a good friend of ours, asked us if we would be afraid to go on a small sailing schooner. It was only one hundred feet across, but we were eager to get on a boat that would take us back to the United States. I was only seventeen years old and I wanted to have a taste of bowling and movies and boyfriends, and I wanted to lead a normal life like other boys and girls. So we went to look at the Potii. When we saw that very, very old boat, we didn't care. The French inspector took a look at the boat and he said we couldn't sail on it because it was too dangerous. We were really upset about that.

Luckily, the French captain didn't give up. He found another boat, a cute, small boat that had been converted from a Navy boat. A few Americans, several crew members, and the animals we brought got on the boat. Just before we left, an old Tahitian man came up to us and said, "Please don't go." We asked him why. He warned us that the Matai Rahi was coming. That meant a terrible hurricane was on the way. Well, we had had enough of Tahiti after six years, so we boarded the boat and we said good-bye. As we left the harbor and went sailing out into the sea, the old man cried and cried because he thought he would never see us again.

After the tenth day at sea, the hurricane hit. It was a terrible storm— the boat went rocking up and down on the waves. It would go up and then crash down again. The water came flooding over the sides. All day long it worsened. The waves kept hitting against the boat. The boat began to tilt back and forth, and the water began to come in. All of the people remained inside the cabin. The water swished on the floor of the cabin and went up one side and down the other. All the people got together and began to pray. The boat had been rocking back and forth for a while when, all of a sudden, it became quiet. We knew then we had gone underwater, we could feel the water pressure above us. I thought, I'm going to die and I'm only seventeen years old. I asked my mother, "Are we going down?"

My mother was very cool. She looked at me and said, "Oh, don't worry. Don't think about it as going down. Water is deep and blue like heaven and the white sands are the same as the white clouds above, the same as heaven. Your hair will become like seaweed and float on the waves. Your teeth will become shiny pearls. Your bones will become coral. Isn't that a pretty way to die?"

I accepted that. I couldn't do anything about it. But by a miracle the boat came shooting up out of the water like a cork, and we were saved! Half of our pigs drowned, though. We butchered them and ate them during the rest of the trip. Also, the ocean water got into our water barrels, so we had to drink salty water. Many, many things happened on that trip, but we finally did arrive in the U.S.

Part Two

In 1976 I planned a trip around the world for one year to spread the message of total communication. I made all the preparations. Before I left, a friend said to me, "You know that guardian angels always watch over children and fools. You be careful." But as I look back, I know I have been a fool!

My first stop was in India. After that I went to southern Africa. We were supposed to stop in Mozambique to transfer from one plane to another. As it happened, Mozambique was hit by terrible weather and we were grounded. I stood in the airport wondering, not knowing, what to do. In Mozambique they really hated white people because of the cruel treatment by the Portuguese in the past.

There were big banners across the walls that said "Yankees go home. Imperialists go home. White people go home."

Carefully, I walked outside with my luggage. A white man came up to me. I admitted to him that I couldn't hear. He wrote a note to me, asking if I were French, German, or British. I told him I was American. He warned me about wearing gold jewelry and about walking alone. I thanked him and took a taxi to a hotel. With four fours to wait until dinner, I rebelled against the man's warning and went outside. The town was dead—not much business or excitement going on. I just strolled around; I felt very safe.

On my way back to the hotel I noticed an alley that seemed to be a good shortcut. So I started to walk through it. Suddenly three men between the ages of eighteen and twenty appeared. One of them put his hand over my mouth, grabbed my arms, and pulled me out of sight. (I envisioned my guardian angel's wings finally being too tired to help me. Now I was obviously a fool; my friend had been right.) The man in the middle took my purse, which contained $200. He took my earrings and the bracelets I had bought for my daughters. Then, they pinned me down. I was sure one was about to rape me. I was trembling all over. The man in the middle started to talk to me. The other two had hold of my hands, but somehow I managed to gesture that I was deaf. He gestured back—You can't hear? He gestured to the other men to get away and leave me alone. I wondered what had happened. Then he gestured to me in international sign that he had a deaf sister. He asked me what I was doing. I explained that I was carrying the message of total communication around the world. Well, his deaf sister was oral and she had never been happy. He spared my life so I could continue my work. He even asked if he could help me to my hotel. I told him I preferred going alone, in spite of my trembling. He knelt down and kissed my hand and said that my angel would take care of me.

When I reached my hotel room, I wept stormily. I realized that if I had not been deaf, I would have been killed. Or if he had not had a deaf sister, I would have been killed. It's such a big world and that was such a small alley.

About a month later, I was in Nigeria. I told my friend the story of what had happened in Mozambique—how terrible it was, what an awful coward I was, and how hard I had cried. He looked at me and said, "You're a coward? Then how did it happen that you stayed here instead of going straight home?"

Some People Just Can't Read

Leon Auerbach

The summer of 1938 was really hot. During that summer I took a trip on a Greyhound bus. I sat next to a middle-aged hearing man. When he started to speak to me, I motioned to him in signs that I couldn't hear. So we just sat there on the bus.

We rode on the bus for hours and hours. Then we stopped at a little roadside store. We got out and stretched a bit. Boy! It was hot. The man who had been sitting next to me walked up to me and handed me a Coke. It was ice cold. I thanked him and I gave a little *nice* sign. That Coke tasted really good. When I had finished it, I went into the store and bought a magazine—a *Saturday Evening Post*.

After a while, everybody got back on the bus. As we rode along I leafed through the magazine. I realized that I had not really thanked the man properly. I wanted to let him know that I really appreciated his kindness. Since I didn't have any paper with me, I decided to use the magazine I had just bought. I wrote on the margin; I can't remember exactly what I said, but it was something like, "Thank you for being very kind, I appreciate the Coke." I gave the magazine to him and I asked him to read the margin. He read it for quite a while. Several minutes passed. Then he smiled at me, folded up the magazine, and put it under his arm. Well, that was the last I saw of my magazine.

Rudi and Me

H. Paul Menkis

I want to tell you a story about Rudi and me. Rudi is a dog, a Doberman Pinscher. Dobermans are black and rust. They are beautiful, big dogs; they're not mean dogs. You can train them for dog shows.

How I got Rudi is a long story. A friend knew that I was thinking about getting a dog and so invited me to go to a dog show. At that show I was most fascinated with the Dobermans. They are such a noble kind of dog. I decided I wanted to buy one. I asked some friends how I should go about picking one. They told me to buy from a dog breeder instead of a pet store. I asked them why and they said I would find the best quality dog from the breeder. So I went to see a man who bred pure Dobermans. The breeder showed me a litter; I was fascinated by all the different puppies. The first one that came up to me was cute, but I never really pick the first thing I see. The breeder picked one for me. I wondered how he knew which one to choose, but I trusted him, so I took the puppy. Do you know how much he charged me? You may think it was cheap because it was a long time ago. Well, it wasn't; that puppy cost $350, and that's the truth.

I took the puppy home with me. I got a book so I could learn how to take care of it. One of my friends also gave me advice about raising the puppy. I was very excited. This little thing was just a baby and, of course, it was awkward. I wanted to train it, but my friend told me only to house-train it. My friend said I should wait until the puppy was older. When I asked why, my friend said, "Let your dog enjoy its puppyhood. Remember when you were growing up? You had a right to enjoy yourself, and when you became an adult, you became more serious. It's the same kind of thing with a dog."

I asked how long I should wait before getting into the serious training. My friend answered, "About eight or nine months. You need to wait until that time. But until then, you just train it not to go to the bathroom in the house and things like that."

During those first eight months I signed to Rudi all the time. I never used my voice. I would whistle for him outside, but that was it. As the time for serious training got closer and closer, I began to notice a funny thing. I think what really happened was instead of my training Rudi, Rudi trained me. That's how things went, anyway.

I'll Stick to My Love for Books

Kathleen Schreiber

I want to tell you about a true experience I had at the Minnesota School for the Deaf when I was thirteen years old. Before I went to that school, I lived in northern Minnesota. This was mostly farm land and there were almost no books or libraries. I loved to read, so when I reached the Minnesota School for the Deaf and saw the big library, I wanted to read all the books. I was excited. My first week there, I took five books back to my dorm room. I started reading, and I read every chance I got.

One Saturday my dorm supervisor came into my room and said, "You can't read all the time. You must circulate more, socialize more." I said, "Well, I've finished cleaning my room and I want to read." She just said, "No."

I tried to sneak away into the reading room. I figured in that room it would be all right to read. But, again, my supervisor said no. I went to talk with a friend, but I still wanted to read. So I looked for a way to read.

One day I was walking home from class and I looked up at our dorm, Tate Hall. There was a big cupola on the top, and I thought if I could get in there, the supervisor would never find me. When I got back to the dorm, I sneaked up to the attic. It was real dark in the attic, but when I looked way up, I could see a light. I thought I should try to climb up to the light. I piled up things so I could reach the ladder. Then I had to climb up to another ladder and open a hatch. The hatch opened into a perfect room. I could see the whole campus from up there. The supervisor would never find me up there. I was really excited. I closed the hatch went back down the ladder, and sneaked back into my room.

The next Saturday morning, and the following four Saturdays, I cleaned my room as usual. Then, I hid some books under my clothes and climbed up the ladder to my secret room. I read until twenty minutes before twelve. Then, I climbed back down and got in line for lunch.

On the fifth Saturday morning, I should have suspected that the supervisor was following me around. I had cleaned my room and when I was finished, I sneaked upstairs to the attic. I thought I could read a couple of books in the hours that I had left. When it was twenty before twelve, I opened the hatch. Right away I noticed that the light was on in the attic. Not only that, the superintendent and my supervisor were standing there looking up at me. The superintendent said, "Please be careful." I looked down at them— they looked so small. There were far away. I said, "Don't worry, don't worry."

I climbed out and looked around my room; I thought this would be the last time I would see my little room. I got on the ladder, closed the hatch, started climbing down, and then realized that the ladder was on a wooden plank that was very unsturdy and thin. The ladder was also thin. I had never noticed that before because I hadn't seen it in the light. I continued my climb down, across the plank to the next ladder (which was a bit bigger), and then down a pole. It was a long, long crawl. I had never realized it before because the lights hadn't been on. Finally, I reached the floor.

The superintendent asked, "Why were you up there?" I told him, "I want to read, but my supervisor won't allow me to read my books." The superintendent asked, "Why?" My supervisor said, "She reads too much." They looked at me, looked up at the hatch, and then the superintendent said, "You can read in my office from now on."

The three of us walked away. Sure enough, after that I always went down to the superintendent's office on Saturday mornings. He made a little reading corner for me with a light and everything. I sat and read every Saturday. I really appreciated that. I finally finished six rows of books in the library, and I never heard one word of criticism about what to read. I hope you all learn to love to read as I did and still do.

CHAPTER 15

Mr. Orman and Susie

May Curtis

Mr. Orman was one of my teachers at the Kansas School for the Deaf (KSD). He was short and thin, and we always thought he was old. He was born in 1900.

My little sister Susie also went to KSD. She would run up and hug me whenever she saw me in the hall. Mr. Orman became really fond of Susie. He would stand in the hall during class changes and wait for her. Susie would run up to him, jump into his arms, and grab him around the waist. She did that almost every day.

One September when we had returned to school, we found out that Mr. Orman had moved to the Arkansas School for the Deaf. We did not see him again for many, many years.

A few years ago, Mr. Orman came to Gallaudet College for a reunion. When he saw me, he asked how Susie was. I told him she was fine and that she was teaching at the Kansas School for the Deaf. And then I said, "You can't pick up my sister anymore. She is all grown up. Perhaps now she can pick you up!"

The Windows of My Life

Mel Carter, Jr.

Many deaf students go to schools for the deaf. Most states have one central residential school, and the deaf students from different areas within the state attend that school. I went to the Virginia School for the Deaf. My mother and father went to that same school. I had many of the same teachers and supervisors that my mother and father had. My mother used to tell me many exciting stories about going to that school; I was really excited to be able to attend there.

When the time came for me to leave for school, my mother and I took the train to Staunton. There was a whole group of deaf boys and girls on the train. It seemed quite a large group from my home area (Hampton) was going to the same school in Staunton. We were all very excited. I was fascinated by all the conversations and signing/talking going on. My excitement for school just elevated. One thing I noticed was that the deaf children's parents who could hear sat together in one area of the train; they never talked to us. But, my mother joined right in with all the young children. She talked and chatted and told us stories.

Every time I took the train to school I observed all those things that were going on, but sometimes I would take the time to look out the windows of the train. I'd watch the scenery pass by me. Sometimes I would fall asleep, but most of the time I'd be wide-eyed. Sometimes I would see something really thrilling. The most thrilling sight was the telephone poles. They appeared to zoom past my window. My eyes would become glued to the rhythm of their appearance. I also liked the symmetry of the wires attached to these poles. Sometimes I'd gaze across at the other side of the train and follow the visual music of the wires on the other side. Occasionally some of the telephone poles were down and my eyes would hit the low key on the ground as the train chugged along. The wire patterns were separated, though sometimes they would come together. I'd follow the horizontal swaying of these wires. Whenever my eyes landed on the ground with a grounded telephone pole, I'd talk to the telephone poles saying, "Please don't go down because when you go down, it hurts my eyes."

Of all the things about residential school life, I remember the train as being very important in my life and other boys' and girls' lives. Sometimes the boys and girls would come up with the funniest stories. One time one of them came up to me and asked me, "Do you know why the man who is sitting over there continues to give the sign of the cross?" I replied, "No, I wouldn't know why, or understand why, because I'm not Catholic." My friend replied, "Because he thinks the telephone poles look like crosses. As he sees them go by, he blesses himself with the sign of the cross . . . one blessing for each telephone pole." Then I understood!

The windows of the school were very impressive. There were rows and rows of windows in each building. Sometimes girls and boys would stand at their dorm windows and would get each other's attention. Then, little loving things could be said between boy and girl. They would wink at each other and make subtle or shy comments to one another. Through these windows they would tell how much they liked one another. (A long time ago, using the I love you handshape was more private, but now such dialogue is quite open.) Sometimes couples had fights through the windows. One time a boy and girl had a terrible argument through one of these windows. The boy got so mad that he put his hand through the window. It was terrible; his hand bled a lot.

Another one of my window memories goes back to when I was five years old. I had a group of friends who were also five years old. There was a group of seven, eight and nine year olds who also stuck together. It seemed that each time we had an important day, or when our groups wanted to go outside and play, it would rain. When it rained, we could not go out. We all had to sit inside or go into a small playroom that was lined with many long windows. When we wanted to tell the rain to stop, we'd get together to try to figure out how to accomplish that. Once, one boy went up to a window and started to bang on it. The other boys and girls started to do the same. Soon all around the room, about sixty students were banging away on the windows. Bang! Bang! Bang! This banging was accompanied by shouts to heaven. We thought maybe if God heard us, we'd get our wish and the rain would go away.

We all adopted the window banging technique. Many times we banged on the windows for snow. We always wanted more snow. If there was more snow, we wouldn't have school the next day. One day we finally got God's cooperation. I think it was when I was about fourteen or fifteen years old. It had snowed a little bit, so all of the boys and girls in school decided to try the banging technique. We screamed and yelled to heaven. Heaven seemed to say okay because it continued to snow all evening and all through the night into the morning.

In the morning the supervisor came in to wake us. She told us to get ready for school. We couldn't believe that school was not canceled after all. We looked out the window. The snow was extremely high. It measured sixteen inches. We were thrilled. We felt sure that school would be closed. We were so excited. We went to the cafeteria for breakfast hoping that school was canceled. My supervisor was deaf and she couldn't hear the radio, so she didn't really know whether school was canceled or not. She waited until another supervisor gave her the word. When this supervisor notified her that school was closed, we all jumped up and down and yelled for joy. We threw things and chanted, "No school." For the first time, the banging had worked . . . were we thrilled. Yes, we were grateful to those windows.

Another important window in my life was at Gallaudet College, which is where I met my wife, Sharon. You know what the two of us did? The two of us would stand by our windows in our dorms, which were located across from each other, and we'd talk to each other endlessly. Later on, of course, we didn't need to communicate through windows.

After we became engaged, I took a train to South Dakota to meet Sharon's family. I got on the train and began to look out one of the train windows. I once again gazed at the telephone poles as they went by. I saw once again the wires of the telephone poles. I thought about all the things that had happened in my life. I was twenty years old and I could remember many things from my childhood. I could recollect the funny stories that occurred on the train, even about the man that blessed himself with the sign of the cross. I began to laugh to myself.

As the train approached South Dakota, I became excited. I knew it was almost time to see Sharon again. I sat in the train. I had to be patient. I could feel my heart beating. When we pulled into the train station, I looked out the window and saw that Sharon was there. I expected her mother to be there, too, but her mother wasn't there. I spotted a man who I concluded was Sharon's brother. The two of them looked so great just standing there. It was time for me to get off the train. As I walked off the train I could see through the window. I took pity on the brother because he didn't know which person I was. I helped him recognize me by signing as I waved and carried my luggage. I got off the train and the first thing I meant to do was hug Sharon. But she pulled away from me and wouldn't let me embrace her. She was timid in front of her brother. She led me over to where her brother was, I shook hands with him and exchanged the "How are you, I am fine." Then we got into the car and drove to their house.

I remember I was nervous about meeting Sharon's mother. Inside, my heart was pounding away like crazy. The first thing I noticed was that Sharon's mother could sign and fingerspell. When we met, she signed, "How are you?"

I was shocked that she could sign. I signed to Sharon, "I didn't know your mother was so good at signing and fingerspelling."

She looked puzzled for a moment, and then she said, "You're right, she can sign and fingerspell." Since Sharon had become accustomed to communicating orally with her mother, she hadn't even realized her mother could sign and fingerspell. Sharon's mother was not skilled, but she did fingerspell most of the time. We could communicate.

We had a feast that night. More and more food was brought before us. Most of the food came from the garden. The family wanted to show me where they had grown that food. They pulled me over to the window and I looked out. Behind the garage was a large garden with many, many vegetables growing in it. I envisioned all the things that had gone into making that garden grow. The plowing and sowing of the seeds, the cultivating, and the care.

Another one of my favorite windows was in my classroom at the Minnesota School for the Deaf. I couldn't believe that I had really become a teacher. I would tell stories, all the stories that I had gotten from the various windows of my life, all the things that were part of my past.

I used to have story-reading time in my class. All the students would gather around me. One day we were reading a story that contained the phrase "you are kidding." I thought that maybe those students understood, but I wanted to double check. I called them up to share in the reading of the story. I asked one boy to read that one phrase.

The boy began to read and when he got to that phrase, he spelled "You're k-i-d-d-i-n-g." I pointed to him and said, "Your spelling is okay, but—k-i-d-d-i-n-g—what does that mean? The boy replied, "Well, I don't know."

I said, "Come on, come on . . . give me a sign for that."

The boy looked at me, his mouth hanging open. He looked at all the students and he looked around. I tried to encourage him by saying again, "Come on, come on, give me a sign for the word." T

he boy started saying, "Well, well . . . it means, it means . . ."

I tried to help him. I covered up the i-n-g and just showed him the word *kid*. He said, "Oh, oh, I know, I know, it means *child*" ((signing kid).

I said, "Umm, huh . . . kid, well, that's right; well what does the whole word mean?"

The boy said, "I don't know." I told him to ask the class. All the students in the class signed that they didn't know either. None of them knew what *kidding* meant.

After a while, one of the boys said, "Oh, maybe it means a father, a big man who grew short and became a kid again."

I just about burst into laughter, but I controlled myself. I asked the class, "Is he right?" They all nodded their heads and looked around in agreement saying, "He's right. He's right." At that moment, I closed my book and I looked out the window. I motioned the students to the window and told them to look. I indicated that out on the street there was a big pile of shoes. "Yes," I said, "There are many, many shoes out there."

The girls and girls gulped that down and ran up to the window. They looked but didn't see anything. Then they questioned me with "Where, where?" I said, "It's out there, there on the street. Look, look out there."

One boy turned around to me and said, "You're lying. Stop fooling."

I responded, "Fine." Then I gathered all the children around me again, got them all seated, and said, "I just told you to look out the window, I was fooling; you know the sign for fooling? That's the same as the phrase you're kidding. They all caught on to the idea of what it was—lying, kidding, fooling. It was the same as some other signs they knew, like teasing and other synonyms. They continued to tell me what it meant.

All of these windows have been really important to me. They are like my eyes. My eyes are the windows of my life. I have learned many different things through my eyes. I've gotten many different stories through them. I have enjoyed looking out through many windows. Windows have been a significant part of my life.

Rich Girl, Poor Girl

Hortense Auerbach

The year 1929 was a really big year across the nation. Wall Street crumbled, many banks closed, thousands of people lost their money, and I lost my hearing. At the same time, movies (which had been silent all along) became talkies.

I lived in a very small town—McGehee, Arkansas. Approximately three thousand people lived there. When I became ill, the family doctor was quite puzzled; he wondered what was wrong with me. No one else in the whole area had that problem. We had no hospital in McGehee, so, finally, the doctor sent some of my blood to a lab in Little Rock. The tests showed that I had spinal meningitis. The doctor acted quickly after he learned the test results. He put a quarantine sign on our house. It was a yellow warning sign that stated no one should enter the house. I had a very contagious disease. All my family had to be innoculated.

I was sick for a long time. Finally, I got well. I didn't know how to walk. I didn't know how to move anymore. I had to learn all those things over again, just like a baby. I had to learn to crawl, sit, and walk. I also became deaf. My family didn't know how to communicate with me. They learned how to fingerspell with the English alphabet from the dictionary. And they taught me how. None of us knew anything about schools for the deaf. We had never heard of them. I was the only deaf person in the whole town.

For the first year, my parents sent me back to public school, in the same class (the fourth grade), and I wasn't happy, of course. I just sat there and twiddled my thumbs. At recess time the children would make fun of me and stick their fingers in their ears. I became quite sensitive and withdrawn, so my parents took me out of the school. I stayed home and read for almost two years. Then my stepfather heard about a school for the deaf in Little Rock. He went to look at the school. When he came home, my parents decided I should go there. At first my mother was really upset about it. I was the only girl in the family; I had three brothers. My mother couldn't imagine having her only daughter away at school. But, for my future she was willing to do it. She contacted the school for the deaf to find out what I needed.

My mother didn't want to take me to school, so my stepfather went with me. We took the train from McGehee all the way to Little Rock. Then we took a streetcar to the school. The buildings were on top of a hill. We grabbed my suitcases and went into the main building.

After we had signed all the papers, I was led into the girls' dorm. I was quite nervous. I looked around and saw hordes of children. They were throwing their arms around. I asked my father what those kids were doing and why they all threw their hands around like that. My father quickly put something in my hand and hurried out of the room. All the girls approached me, one-by-one, and asked me what I had in my hand. Well, I opened my hand and saw a ten-dollar bill! They were all amazed! That was a lot of money, and it was mine. I had never had more than five cents before in my whole life.

I held the money tightly while the little girls tried to communicate with me. I held it for what seemed to be about an hour. Then the supervisor came in to get me. My stepfather was waiting in another room. He came up to me and said, "Give the money to me." I said, "What?" "Give me the money." So I opened up my hand and he took the ten dollars. He gave me nothing in return. I had been wealthy for a short time, then I was back to being poor.

Church Experiences

Nathie Couthen

I grew up in a large family—I have eight sisters and one brother. My parents took us to church regularly. When I was seven and eight, my mother and father didn't like the idea of leaving me at home alone, so they forced me to go to church. They also forced me to join the children's choir. Imagine that!

The children stood in rows when it was time to sing. When the conductor would raise his hand, I would open my book with everybody else. I looked at the people next to me from the corner of my eye and mouthed the words with them. I opened my mouth to la, la, la when I saw the person on my right la, la, la. When that person turned a page, I turned a page. I would constantly be looking back and forth with my eyes, mouthing the words. When everyone closed their books, I closed mine, too, and we'd all file out and take our seats.

I sang in the choir for about four or five years. Then finally, I got fed up and told my mother I didn't want to participate anymore; after all, I could not hear. People knew that I couldn't sing. My lip movements were different from everybody else's. My mother finally agreed. She was willing to let me just sit in the congregation. I was glad about that.

I was happy not to be in the choir. I would sit and watch the preacher for a while, and then I would make up different games for myself since I could not understand what the preacher was saying. I would sit quietly and watch the people in the congregation. Soon, though, I became bored. I told my mother that many times. Finally she decided that I wouldn't have to go to church anymore. I could stay home alone. I was relieved!

How I Learned about My Deafness

H. Paul Menkis

How I learned I became deaf is a long story. When I was born, I could hear. I can remember hearing when I was an infant. I can remember especially because there were two noises that really bothered me—the lawnmower and the telephone. Both of those noises always woke me up from my naps.

When I was about two, two-and-a-half, I became very ill with polio. I was lucky that it didn't leave me with any other handicaps. All polio did to me was ruin the nerves connected to my ears. My parents later explained to me that for two weeks I was in a coma. When I became better I was still pretty weak, and I had to go through rehabilitation exercises.

After I had recovered, I never really noticed that I couldn't hear anymore. I just forgot all about it. But one thing did strike me as being strange. I'd watch my uncle mowing the lawn. I would watch him and get this strange feeling, you know, that for some reason I just hated this lawnmower. But I couldn't remember why. Sometimes I would look at the telephone and get that same feeling— that I just abhorred that telephone. But I couldn't remember why. I used to think about that quite a lot, the lawnmower and the telephone, but eventually it all faded from my awareness.

The strangest thing I noticed was that my parents took turns moving their mouths up and down. I also watched my aunt and uncle do the same thing. So I started to imitate them, you know, just babbling. I didn't have any words or sentences, I just moved my mouth and tried to be involved in whatever they were doing. They would react to me as if they were embarrassed; I don't know if they thought I was cute or stupid or what, but anyway, it all made me wonder. I'd be even more puzzled when they wouldn't be looking at each other but they still knew when to move their mouths. Or else one person would talk and the others would turn and know where to look.

One day I tried an experiment. I turned around and waited to see if I knew when and where to turn. I tried several different directions and never did I know what was going on. But they sure knew how to do it, all of their eyes darted to whoever was moving their lips. I experimented with this, too; I moved my mouth and, sure enough, everyone looked at me.

I continued to imitate people like this, and finally, I asked my mother and father about this lip movement thing. I knew it had to do with communication but I didn't understand that it came in through the ear. I thought that somehow you listened through the mouth just as you expressed yourself out of the mouth.

I asked my parents, "Will I be able to talk like you?" My father answered, "Oh, sure, later on you will be able to talk." So I knew I would be able to talk when I grew up, but I didn't really want to wait. I also asked my aunt and uncle. I saw that I had put them on the spot. They froze for a second and didn't know how to explain it to me. I knew something was up, but basically they told me the same thing—"When you grow up, you will be able to talk." Well, I continued thinking about all this.

I noticed that when I went running out the front door, the door would slam behind me and I could hear it. That was one sound I could hear. Also, I was rather naughty with the toilet seat. I liked to pick it up and let it fall; I'd lift it up and whack it down because it made a loud noise that I could hear. But voices, airplanes, and cars, no way; the sound had to be loud and I had to be right next to it. I used to play by slamming the doors and slamming the toilet seat. And then, one day I started to think about those two noises they made, and once again I asked my mother and father about this. Again, they told me the same thing, which they continued telling me until I was seven years old.

What happened then was this. One day I was watching someone mow the lawn. It still bothered me, as always, and I asked myself why. I knew I hated it when I was younger. I remembered that. And another thing—the telephone. I remember it used to frighten me so terribly, I hated that, too. I hated the phone and I hated the lawnmower. I just continued to think about it—refusing to give up. Finally it came to me. I remembered how those noises bothered me when I was a baby, how those two noises used to wake me up and frighten me. After I became sick, that stopped happening, but I never put two and two together. This time though, I confronted my mother.

"Do you remember, Mom, that before I was sick I was afraid of noises and I hated the telephone? Do you remember where the phone was in the hallway? I remember from when I was two-and-a-half how much I hated the phone and how much it scared me. Whenever I had to go through the hall and pass that telephone, I would walk along, hugging the wall, keeping my eyes on the phone every second until I got safely past it, and then I would scram. I remember that well. And another thing, Mom, I stayed away from that lawnmower. I just kept away from loud noises.

"And remember all those times when I asked you about whether I would be able to talk or not? I never connected the fact that the noises from the lawnmower and phone had disappeared with whether I could talk or not. You always told me that when I grew up I would be able to talk. What's going on?"
My mother finally realized that it was time to deal with this, so she sat me down and she explained the word deaf. She said to me, "Remember when you were sick, when you were a baby, about two-and-a-half?"

"Yes, I can remember. It's pretty amazing how much I can remember from that age."

"Well," Mother said, "Yes, you were very, very sick, and that illness destroyed the nerves that led to your ears. You had a horrible fever and your body temperature went way up. I had to pack you in ice and take care of you constantly. But it didn't help; no matter how well we took care of you, it was useless. The fever destroyed the nerves in your ears."

"You mean I . . ."

And Mother said, "Well, maybe in the future you will talk."

I think my mother, whether consciously or unconsciously, was basing her hopes on hearing aids because at that time researchers were making a lot of progress in hearing aid technology. But really, she should have told me. I wish she had told me that I was deaf. Maybe I could have learned different ways to communicate, and I could have learned things just like anyone else. I remember at that time I became very angry. I felt that a lot of my time—from ages two-and-a-half to seven—had been wasted. All that time I had learned nothing.

So please, I want to warn all you people: if you know a child who has become deaf, tell that child right away. Don't pull the wool over anyone's eyes.

CHAPTER 16

A Summer in Los Angeles

Don G. Pettingill

I became deaf at the age of five. I thought nothing of it because my father was hard of hearing. I had eight brothers and sisters. Whenever I felt sorry for myself and quarreled with them, my sisters and brothers would say "Your deafness is nothing, you're just like your father."

My mother, just like all mothers, felt bad about my deafness. She especially felt bad saying, "My son is deaf." She was always looking for a way for me to regain my hearing. Once my mother took me to an Indian reservation to see an Indian medicine man. All the Indians gathered around while the medicine man put snake oil on my ears. They started jumping around and hollering and carrying on. I understood nothing, and my hearing did not improve at all.

Another time Mother took me to a chiropractor who twisted me around and jerked my neck. For one year I went to that chiropractor, and I really suffered from his ministrations. But, I didn't regain my hearing.

As a last resort, my mother sent me to my aunt and uncle who lived in Los Angeles, California. They had joined a big church. They had told my mother, "If Don came to Los Angeles we would pray in the church. Then, Don would hear again." My mother must have believed them because I went to Los Angeles to stay with my aunt and uncle. The first Sunday morning I was there, we went to church. I was really impressed with the size of the congregation. I sat and twiddled my thumbs during the service. I couldn't understand anything. The next morning my aunt took me to the church and dropped me off. I went into a room filled with people. I was the only young boy there. I couldn't understand what was going on. All at once a man near me jumped up and started wriggling around on the floor. I stared at him, and I started to get scared. I elbowed the man next to me and asked, "What's the matter with him?" He chuckled and told me that the fellow was filled with the Holy Spirit. I thought, "Wow, it must hurt!" The next morning, Tuesday, my aunt dropped me off at church again. I started to open the door, but I couldn't make myself go inside—I was too scared. Instead. I decided to explore Los Angeles.

Every morning for two weeks, my aunt would drop me off at that church, and every day I would wander around the city of Los Angeles until it was time to go home. If my aunt suspected anything, she never let on.

There were so many things to see in Los Angeles. One day I noticed a junk dealer in a horse-drawn wagon going through the alleys. He was picking up junk from trash cans. I asked someone what he did with all that junk and was told that he sold it. I thought that would be a good way for me to make money, so I started going through the alleys; foraging through the trash cans; and collecting bottles, wire, and old clothing. When the junk dealer came by the next time, I sold everything to him. He gave me one hundred pennies. This really excited me; money of my own! I began working extra hard collecting old newspapers and anything else I could. Soon I had enough money to buy a little red wagon. This enabled me to collect more junk, which meant more money. I was proud of my little business. I started going farther and farther away from home, looking for more riches in the alleys. I would be exhausted when I finally got home. Sometimes when I came to a steep hill, I would get in my wagon and coast all the way down, getting a little rest on the way. But it was wild! Sometimes the wagon would go so fast I would pray that I wouldn't get hit by a car as I shot across an intersection. Fortunately I never got hit, but there were many near-misses. However, my fear of getting hit didn't stop me from coasting down hills whenever I could.

I really learned a lot of things that summer in Los Angeles. I learned how to be honest and straight with people. And I learned how to ask. One of my friends taught me how to sneak into a rich woman's yard and steal figs from her tree. I liked figs, so every chance I could, I would go in and get some figs and eat them. Well, one day while I was picking some figs from the tree, someone grabbed me and turned me around. It was the rich woman. She had a stern expression. She asked me why I was stealing her figs. I understood what she said but pretended I couldn't. I told her I was deaf. She was taken aback, and said, "Why, you poor little boy!" She started patting me on the back and being nice, then she asked kindly why I was stealing her figs. This time I answered her: "Well, I'm hungry."

She replied, "You don't have to steal; why don't you just ask?"

I said, "Oh, if I had asked, would you have given me the figs?"

She said, "Of course! I have lots of figs, there's no need for you to steal." So I learned how important it was to be honest and to ask.

I learned something about people during my stay in Los Angeles. I would spend all day wandering around with my little red wagon. Sometimes I would get lost, and then I would need to ask for help. I always carried a little card in my pocket that had my address. Some people were really nice and would try to help by giving me directions, which I didn't always understand. Others would go out of their way to drive me home. Still others would try giving me directions, but when I could not understand them after several attempts, they would get frustrated and tell me to go away. There were so many different types of people. I learned how not to be afraid; if I got lost I could always find help from someone.

I also learned about bullies. I learned not to let them frighten or threaten me. On one of my trips with my little red wagon, a gang of boys started following me around. They screamed insults at me. I knew what they were doing from the expressions on their faces. They were especially mean because I couldn't hear. One day they all gathered around me in a circle so that I couldn't get away. I was scared, but I just stood there, not moving. They started taunting me and I just stood my ground, looking at them and trying not to show my fear. I was not sure what I should do. There was one boy right in front of me, and I knew he was the leader. I stared right into his eyes, let out a wild yell, and ran at him. I punched him in the nose and knocked him down. I could see he was scared, and I knew I had won the respect of the other boys. They decided then that I should be their leader. Can you imagine that, a deaf kid leading a bunch of hearing kids? That group became my first sign language class. I taught them many signs. This was also my first deaf awareness class. I explained all about deafness—the frustrations and everything. Two of those gang members are still good friends of mine.

Oh, it was a very interesting summer. I also learned about hypocrites. At the end of the summer the church had a big revival. Most of the church staff knew that I didn't attend church at all after the first two days, but the officials saw a chance to prove that their church could work miracles. I was coached to go up on the stage and shout into the microphone, "Praise the Lord, I can hear better than I did!" I knew that wasn't true, but I couldn't resist the temptation to be the center of attention. There must have been five thousand people watching me, and I still remember how the church erupted. People started screaming, crying, and carrying on. Several women of the church kept coming up and hugging me and crying, and I almost got smothered in their ample bosoms. I do believe my simple declaration helped raise $100,000 for the church that day. That's hypocrisy for you.

There must be a moral to this story. I think it could be best described as, "Keep an open mind and dare to be different!"

Spelling

May Curtis

My mathematics teacher at the Kansas School for the Deaf was Edward Foltz. He had graduated from Gallaudet in 1915. One day he went to the drugstore. When the manager saw Foltz, he got his attention because he needed help. One of the boys from KSD was in the store. The boy had written a note that said, "I want Sunday." The manager didn't know what he meant. Foltz thought for a while, and then said, "Oh, he means he came here for some ice cream. He means sundae."

Foltz knew that many of the students at KSD were terrible spellers. So from then on, he decided to do something about it. He would look around at the boys and girls talking to each other and would ask them what the word was for different signs. For example, if they signed crazy stomach, he would ask what the word for that was. Sometimes he would give them a word and they would have to show him the sign.

Whenever we had five or ten minutes left before the end of class, Foltz would bang on the table to get our attention. He would say, "We are going to have a spelling list—ten words. Number your papers one to ten." Then he would say, "I want you to spell out the word for gym."

"We know gym, g-y-m."

"No, you have to spell out the entire word on paper. Next, think of another word for the sign exercise—not the word exercise itself, but something that starts with a c."

"C? Oh, calisthenics," we answered.

We would go through several signs and words like these. One word I especially liked was for the sign with arms on the hips. It is akimbo. Some girls and boys did not like this kind of spelling class, but I found that it taught us to spell correctly. Now I wonder why schools for the deaf don't have spelling bees. I think it is a good idea. Do you?

My Experiences in School

Carolyn McCaskill

I grew up in Mobile, Alabama. I attended a public high school. At that time, 1963, there were no interpreters in my school. I became very, very frustrated. I depended on my hearing friends for information about what was going on in class. School became so frustrating that one day I just gave up. I told my mother I didn't want to go to that school anymore. I wanted to transfer to the Alabama School for the Deaf. My mother finally gave in, and my sister (who's also deaf) and I transferred to the Alabama School for the Deaf.

My sister and I felt a little awkward at our new school. We didn't know any sign language and there were no sign language classes at the school. We had to pick up signing by associating with the deaf students. The Alabama School for the Deaf was a segregated school. It was only for black deaf children. The students' educational values were very, very low. My sister and I really never had to study because we had very good backgrounds from the public schools, even though we had missed a lot of information in school.

I did not have any role models. I never had heard of a successful black deaf person. I did not know any black deaf teachers, or principals, or successful business people. Most of the black deaf people who graduated from the Alabama School for the Deaf went to work in factories or laundries, or they became custodians or janitors. I realized that I did not want that to happen to me.

Fortunately, the Alabama School for the Deaf was forced to integrate in 1968. Integration of black and white students was a whole new experience. Educational values became very high. I learned so much, it was like being in a different world.

I learned about Gallaudet College. Before, I had never even heard of Gallaudet College. I remember asking some deaf white teachers if blacks could enter Gallaudet. The teachers said of course. I asked one teacher to show me the Tower Clock (the Gallaudet yearbook). My jaw fell when I saw pictures of African students. My teacher assured me I could get into Gallaudet. I said, "Me? No way! I'm too dumb." I just thought that all black deaf students were dumb. The teacher said, "No, you can do it. You just have to study hard."

I asked her how I could improve my English. She said, "By reading."

I said, "Reading? I don't like that, it would be really boring."

"That's the only way you're going to improve yourself," she replied.

So, I read and I read. When my teacher asked me what I wanted to become in the future, I told her a teacher or a counselor. I wanted to help other deaf children. My teacher encouraged me. I had several good white deaf role models. My teachers encouraged me to study hard. They said if I studied hard I would pass the Gallaudet exam. My goal became to study hard.

I passed the Gallaudet Entrance Exam and so did my sister. We both went to Gallaudet. Being at Gallaudet was an eye-opening experience. I met African students, Chinese students, and Russian and German students. I was so happy my first year at Gallaudet. I wrote home often to describe to my mother my different experiences at Gallaudet. I really enjoyed my years at Gallaudet. My best year was 1976—that's when I became Miss Gallaudet. I really felt that was the biggest achievement of my life at Gallaudet.

My sister and I both completed all five years at Gallaudet, and we graduated in 1977. By that time, I had decided to enter the graduate school; I wanted to become a counselor rather than a teacher. I attended the graduate school for two years, and I graduated in 1979. Then I applied for work at the Model Secondary School for the Deaf (MSSD). I worked there for two years as a dorm counselor. And then in the fall of 1981 I became a school counselor at MSSD.

I feel that I have accomplished a lot. But I'm still not finished with my goals. Every time I've succeeded in attaining one goal, I set another one. My next goal is to get my Ph.D. someday. I believe that you can succeed if you set your mind to it; then you can indeed attain your goals.

Born Deaf and Free

Frances M. Parsons

During the year 1976, I traveled around the world to fight against oralism and to explain the value of total communication. I visited many countries. When I look back now, I wonder if it was worth all my time, effort, strength, and health; and I wonder if I accomplished my work. Many countries indicated that they appreciated gaining an understanding of the meaning and value of total communication.

While I was in Nigeria, I stayed in the home of Gabriel Adepoju. Adepoju is deaf, and he is the principal of a school. One night we had a long talk. He asked me if I was writing a story about my travel experiences. I told him I was writing a diary and that I sent it to Gallaudet every month. I also said that maybe someday I would write a book. He told me that I should write something very strong that had a lot of impact. "Many people can't read a book, but something very short and strong will have more impact," he said. That night I went to bed at about midnight. I felt restless. At about one o'clock in the morning I woke up. I had a lot of ideas in my head. I got a pencil and some paper and started writing. Before I knew it, it was five o'clock in the morning. I looked at what I had done, then I put it aside, turned the lights off, and went to sleep.

The next morning I looked at the poem I had written. I decided to call it *Born Deaf and Free*. It is a long poem. The first part of it goes like this:

Born Deaf and Free

Bells!
Bells! Bells! Bells!
Who can hear the bells?

The Hearing
The Hard of Hearing
The Partially Hearing

I am deaf, congenitally and profoundly deaf.
Born deaf, stubborn and free.
I was born to a hearing mother and a hearing father but they granted me
the greatest gift ever bestowed—Love, Pride and Independence.
I was their beautiful mistake.

Happiness came first.
Education came next.
Speech came last.

My mother and father could hear and they heard the pleas of the deaf.

Bells!
Bells! Bells! Bells!
They gave me a bell of confidence
> *a bell of happiness*
> *a bell of harmony*
> *a bell of hope*

Through heavenly communication of godgiven and godsent dancing
hands and prancing fingers.

Bells!
Bells! Bells! Bells!
Who can hear the bells?

So far, my poem has been translated into eight different languages.

MEET THE STORYTELLERS

A: Doctorate earned after the original book was published.
H: Honorary doctorate given after the original book was published.
D: Year of passing.

Hubert Anderson, Jr. (D. 1997) Affectionately known as "Mr. Basketball" during his athletic career at Gallaudet College, Hubert Anderson, Jr., is on his way to achieving legendary status in the American Athletic Association of the Deaf. His most notable accomplishments have occurred through his involvement with four different clubs—Potomac Silents Club, Diplomat Athletic Association of the Deaf, Block "G" Club at Gallaudet, and Carolina Athletic Association of the Deaf in North Carolina. As the head basketball coach, he guided all of these club teams to national tournaments. Two of the teams won national championships while the other two won respectable second- and third-place finishes.

Hubert is also well-known for his success as an administrator on the campus of a hearing college. He was head of the post office at the American University in Washington, D.C. He supervised a staff of fifty-nine postal workers. Despite his deafness, he was hired from among a long list of applicants and he proceeded to develop, in just one year, a campus postal system that has been emulated by many local colleges.

In May 1983, Hubert completed his bachelor of arts degree in history at Gallaudet. He is presently pursuing a master's degree in the area of deafness and rehabilitation at New York University.

Heimo I. Antila (D. 1998) Heimo I. Antila has been spinning quips, puns, jokes, and anecdotes for many years. He was born four months after his parents arrived in the United States from

Finland. After his hearing was affected by a bout with measles at the age of two, Heimo's youth was divided between two worlds—the ethnic Finnish environment of his home and the American deaf culture of his schools. He attended the American School for the Deaf and matriculated at Gallaudet College. He spent two years as a dorm counselor at Kendall School.

Many of Heimo's anecdotes are based on real-life experiences, which he often laces with humor. His collection of stories include tales from his family life, his school life, his life-long career as a union printer, and his travels in America and abroad.

Heimo served as the president of the District of Columbia chapter of the Gallaudet College Alumni Association for four years. He also participated in the Ole Jim Fund Drive.

Hortense Auerbach (D. 2015) Up until she was nine years old, Horty Auerbach could listen to a wind-up Victrola. That was her favorite pastime—she loved sentimental ballads! When she became deaf after a bout with spinal meningitis, her whole world changed. Her parents knew nothing about schools for the deaf, so until she was twelve, she remained at home. She spent most of her time reading. When she was twelve, her stepfather too her to the Arkansas School for the Deaf, and she remained there for four years.

After graduating from Gallaudet College in 1940, Horty went back to the Arkansas school to teach. She taught for one year, and then married her college sweetheart, Leon Auerbach. They moved to Arizona, and from Arizona to Massachusetts, and then back to the Gallaudet campus. After the last of their three children started school, Horty returned to work. She taught reading in the Tutorial Center at Gallaudet for several years. She later became the director of the Tutorial Center and remained in that position until her retirement in 1980.

Horty now keeps busy doing volunteer work at the National Association of the Deaf (NAD), editing two papers, and working for her church. During her spare time, she takes care of her four grandchildren who reside in the Washington area.

Leon Auerbach (D. 1991) Leon Auerbach, deaf son of deaf parents and brother of a deaf sister, is a product of the New York School for the Deaf (Fanwood). He graduated from Gallaudet College with the class of 1940 and obtained his first teaching position at the Arizona School for the Deaf. During World War II he worked as a research associate in the Radiation Laboratory at the Massachusetts Institute of Technology in Cambridge. He came to Gallaudet as an instructor in the fall of 1944, and has been there ever since.

In 1963, Leon became chairman of the Gallaudet mathematics department. He conducted seven summer mathematics institutes for teachers of the deaf, and obtained funding from the National Science Foundation and the Bureau of Education of the Handicapped in the U.S. Office of Education.

Leon has been active in several deaf organizations. He served as president of the Metropolitan Washington Association of the Deaf, as well as the Maryland Association of the Deaf. He is married to his Gallaudet classmate, E. Hortense Henson. They have three children and several grandchildren.

Bernard Bragg (H) If Bernard Bragg is no mean whiz at telling a good story, that is because he has never been known to be dull. In addition to his accomplishments as a storyteller, he is a well-known actor, mime, director, teacher, playwright, and TV personality. He is a graduate of Gallaudet College, and he has studied with Marcel Marceau, the internationally known mime.

As an actor, Bernard has starred in such recent hits as *And Your Name is Jonah* and *The White Hawk*. As a mime he has originated many famous routines; as a director and playwright he has directed and co-authored the recently acclaimed play, *Tales from a Clubroom*, and the comedy,

That Makes Two of Us. His past achievements include appearing in a weekly TV show, *The Quiet Man*, which was produced by KQED in San Francisco, being a co-founder of the National Theatre of the Deaf, and serving as a goodwill ambassador of the United States Department of State.

This born raconteur livens up his stories with such flair that he always casts a spell over his audiences.

S. Melvin Carter, Jr.
S. Melvin Carter, Jr. (known as Mel) heads the Communicative Skills of the NAD. He hails from Virginia and graduated from Virginia School for the Deaf and Blind (VSDB). He calls the United States his home because he worked and continues to work with programs and people in various parts of the country. He was born to deaf parents who also attended VSDB, so he got an early glimpse of deaf culture through early contact with deaf people and deaf clubs and social functions.

Mel cherishes his days as a teacher at the Minnesota School for the Deaf in Faribault, Minnesota, as Educational Director at the Central North Carolina School for the Deaf (now located in Greensboro), and as a member of the National Center on Deafness staff at California State University, Northridge (CSUN). One highlight of his career was the opportunity to work with people of other countries, including Guam and Japan.

He is a traveling lecturer on topics such as deaf awareness, teaching sign language, ASL and interpreters, ASL and teachers, and deaf people and interpreters. He also conducts workshops for specialized groups e.g., sign language teachers and interpreters. He heads the National Symposium on Sign Language Research and Teaching and the National Consortium of Programs for the Training of Sign Language Instructors.

Mel is a graduate of Gallaudet College (1967), and the National Leadership Training Program at CSUN (1975). He is now in the dissertation stage of his doctoral studies in educational administration at Brigham Young University in Provo, Utah.

He enjoys reading, meeting people, and going to the theatre (especially to see captioned/subtitled movies). His avocation is emceeing. He also does some woodworking. His favorite pastime is being with his wife, Sharon Heiydt Carter. Together they enjoy life in their home in Laurel, Maryland, with their four pets—Sharmelia, a sixteen-year-old Chihuahua who is deaf; Whoo, a three-year-old white cat with black ears and tail; Kitty, a tabby cat who adopted them; and Ohren a two-and-half-year-old hearing ear German Shepherd.

Edward E. Corbett, Jr., Ph.D.

(D. 2012)

Ed Corbett, a native of Shreveport, Louisiana, began his professional career as a graphic arts teacher at the Louisiana State School for the Deaf. Since leaving his home state, Ed has been actively involved in programs and services that benefit the deaf community. He received his B.A. from Gallaudet College and his M.A. from the California State University at Northridge. He was the first deaf recipient of a Ph.D. from Gallaudet College.

Ed has had an impressive career in deaf education. In addition to his years as a teacher, he served as the communication-community education coordinator at the Margaret S. Sterck School for the Hearing Impaired in Newark, Delaware; the assistant superintendent at the Maryland School for the Deaf at the Frederick and Columbia campuses; and an intern with the U.S. House of representatives' Committee on Education and Labor, where he monitored compliance with Section 504 of the Rehabilitation Act of 1973 and helped draft the Interpreter Training Act, a part of Public Law 95-602. Dr. Corbett is currently the director of the National Academy of Gallaudet College. He has several publications to his credit, including the recently published *Teachers of the Deaf: Descriptive Profiles*, which he co-authored with Dr. Carl J. Jensema.

Nathie Couthen (Marbury)

(A; D. 2013)

Nathie Couthen is the ninth and only deaf child in a hearing family of ten children. Her parents sent her to the

Western Pennsylvania School for the Deaf in Pittsburgh. She graduated from Gallaudet College and received her M.A. from California State University at Northridge.

Nathie taught American history, social studies, and life adjustment at the American School for the Deaf in West Hartford, Connecticut. She then moved to the Washington, D.C. area, where she taught home economics at the Kendall Demonstration Elementary School (KDES). After teaching for five years, she became the Communication Specialist/Sign Language at KDES.

Nathie resides in Riverdale, Maryland, with her two teenage daughters.

Florence B. Crammatte (D. 2000) Widely known as an organizer and innovator, Florence B. Crammatte is currently the co-chairperson, with her husband, of the fundraising campaign to restore Gallaudet's 19th-century gymnasium for use as the Alumni House. As national president of Phi Kappa Zeta sorority (1960-67), she established its biannual newsletter, *The Phi Kappa Zetan*, and the Phi Kappa Zeta Woman of the Year Award. Her other literary efforts include editing Rev. Guilbert C. Braddock's book, *Notable Deaf Persons*, and editing a monthly newsletter for an employees' association. Florence's first employment after graduation from Gallaudet College was as a museum assistant with the Hispanic Society of America in New York City. She taught for a short time at the Louisiana School for the Deaf and entered federal civil service during World War II. Her longest position was with the Plant Industry Station, U.S. Department of Agriculture, as a statistical assistant. Upon retirement from USDA in 1972, she worked part-time in the Office of Alumni and Public Relations at Gallaudet College. She is now retired again but continues to do volunteer work.

Florence has been an active member of the Gallaudet College Alumni Association. She served as the first chairperson of the GCAA's Laurent Clerc Cultural Fund Committee (1967-1973). Under her guidance, the LCCF committee has made many contributions to the

Gallaudet campus, including the presentation of a bronze cast of the original small model of the Daniel Chester French statue of Thomas Hopkins Gallaudet and Alice Cogswell, and the provision of seed money for numerous cultural projects.

May Curtis
(D. 2003)
May Curtis is a graduate of the Kansas School for the Deaf. She had two excellent role models at KSD—Edward Foltz and James Orman. She still remembers their signmaking and storytelling skills.

During the Depression years, May attended Gallaudet College. Soon after she graduated, she found a position as a teacher of clothing and physical education at the South Dakota School for the Deaf. During World War II, Uncle Sam called May and other Rosies (the riveters) to Akron, Ohio, to work in an aircraft factory.

After the war, May and her husband, Ivan, moved to Washington, D.C., where she worked for the federal government for thirty-four years. She is now retired from work, but is quite active in the community. She is still on the go in the cultural world of Washington, D.C. May is also a volunteer worker at Gallaudet College.

Robert Davila, Ph.D.
(H)
Robert (Bob) Davila was born into a Spanish-speaking family in San Diego, California, in 1932. He became deaf at the age of eight as a result of an attack of spinal meningitis. Soon thereafter, he began his education at the California School for the Deaf (Berkeley), where he learned English and played sports. After graduating from CSD, Bob went on to Gallaudet College and became the only member of his family to go on to postsecondary education. His Gallaudet years were consumed by studies, although he did have time to work for *The Buff and Blue* as a writer and sports editor.

Following his graduation in 1953, Bob married Donna Ekstrom. They moved to New York, where their two sons, Brian and Brent, were born.

Bob taught at the New York School for the Deaf. He began his teaching career in the elementary school; he went on to teach social studies and math to high school students before becoming supervisor of the elementary school. During this time, Bob studied at the City University of New York. He received his master's degree in 1963. He continued his studies at Syracuse University and received his doctorate in educational technology in 1972. He and his family then moved to Washington, D.C., where he joined the faculty of the Gallaudet College Department of Education. Two years later he became the director of Kendall School. He managed the program until 1978, when he was appointed Vice-President of Pre-College Programs.

Bob's hobbies include tennis, raising tomatoes, and, of course, telling stories like "A Lucky Christmas."

Bob served as the Office of Special Education and Rehabilitative Services Assistant Secretary at the Department of Education, as the National Technical Institute for the Deaf President, and as Gallaudet University President.

Gilbert Eastman
(H; D. 2006)
Gilbert Eastman, a graduate of Gallaudet College, has long been associated with theatre at Gallaudet College. After he earned his master's degree in drama from Catholic University, he was instrumental in starting the drama department at Gallaudet College. Gil was a founding member of the National Theatre of the Deaf, and it was there he received much of his professional theatre training. After leaving NTD, he returned to Gallaudet College, where he developed two courses, *Sign Language Translation for the Theatre* and *Visual Gestural Communication as a Sign Language Base* (formerly *Nonverbal Communication*). He has traveled both nationally and internationally to conduct workshops in Visual Gestural Communication. He has written and produced (at Gallaudet College) two plays, *Sign Me Alice* (published) and *Laurent Clerc: A Profile*.

Gil has conducted extensive research on Laurent Clerc, who was the first, and possibly the most important, deaf teacher in the United States. His research and subsequent play have led him to lecture about Laurent Clerc at numerous sites. Mr. Eastman is currently a professor of theatre and chairman of the Theatre Arts Department at Gallaudet College. He resides in Crofton, Maryland, with his wife and two daughters.

Jack Gannon (H)
Jack Gannon, director of Alumni and Public Relations at Gallaudet College, was born November 23, 1936, in West Plains, Missouri. He became deaf at the age of eight as a result of spinal meningitis, entered the Missouri School for the Deaf in 1946, and graduated in 1954. From 1954 to 1959, he was a student at Gallaudet College, majoring in education and devoting a great deal of his spare time to his two loves: football and journalism. As editor of the college newspaper, *The Buff and Blue*, he won first class ratings for the paper from the Associated College Press. He co-captained the varsity football squad in 1957, was president of the Alpha Sigma Pi fraternity, and served as editor of the 1959 *Tower Clock*, the college yearbook.

Following graduation from Gallaudet, Jack was an instructor in graphic arts and a coach at the Nebraska School for the Deaf. In 1967 he was honored as "Coach of the Year" by Omaha's WOW-TV when his eight-man football team had an undefeated season. Jack returned to Gallaudet College in 1968 to serve as director of Alumni Relations. In 1971, when the alumni and public information offices were reorganized and combined into the new Office of Alumni and Public Relations, he became director of that overall operation. This office is responsible for the alumni program, publications, public relations, the new national information center, and the college visitors program.

Jack is the author of *Deaf Heritage: A Narrative History of Deaf America*, recently published by the NAD. He is married to the former Rosalyn Lee of Winston-Salem. They live in Silver Spring, Maryland, with their two children, Jeff and Christy.

Mervin D. Garretson
(H; D. 2013)
Mervin D. Garretson is frequently referred to as the "Father of the Junior NAD." He grew up on a cattle ranch near a small town in northern Wyoming. He became profoundly deaf at the age of five from spinal meningitis. After spending eleven years at the Colorado School for the Deaf, he entered Gallaudet College. He graduated from Gallaudet in 1947. He later received his master's degree from the University of Wyoming and he did doctoral work at the University of Maryland.

After three years as a classroom teacher at the Maryland School for the Deaf, Mervin moved to Montana. He obtained a teaching position at the Montana School for the Deaf, and later became principal of that school. It was during his Montana years that he became interested in the concept of a Junior NAD. He was appointed its first national director in 1960. After twelve years as a principal, Mervin returned east to assume the position of associate professor of education at Gallaudet College.

He also served as executive director of the Council of Organizations Serving the Deaf, and as principal of the Model Secondary School for the Deaf on the Gallaudet campus. At the present time, Mervin is special assistant to the president of Gallaudet College.

Mervin has been very active in the NAD, having held every office in that organization, including president. In addition, he has been active in the World Federation of the Deaf since 1967, when he was elected to the WFD Board of Directors. He is married to Carol Kaull and they have five daughters.

Francis C. Higgins
(D. 2000)
Francis C. Higgins attended the Flemington (N.J.) Grammar School, although he has been deaf since the age of three. Following his graduation in 1927, he studied at the New Jersey School for the Deaf. He graduated in 1931, and from there he matriculated at Gallaudet College. He received his bachelor of science degree in 1936. He took graduate

courses at Rutgers University and received his master of science degree in 1938. From 1938 to 1947, Francis taught at the Kentucky School for the Deaf. Since then he has been teaching at Gallaudet College. He has also served as chairman of the chemistry department.

While teaching in Kentucky, Francis was instrumental in establishing the Kentucky chapter of the Gallaudet College Alumni Association. He became its first president. Since 1949, Francis has served as lay leader of the Baptist Church of the Deaf in Washington, D.C. He conducts church services and church school classes. He has conducted similar services for the Baptist students of the Ephphatha Bible class at Gallaudet. College. Currently he is the coordinator of Volunteer Services for the Deaf, an organization formed by Washington churches for the deaf in 1967.

Francis has written a number of articles and has received a number of honors. He is a member of the American Association for the Advancement of Science, the American Chemical Society, the National Science Teachers Association, the Foundation for Science and the Handicapped,

and the Convention of American Instructors for the Deaf, to name just a few.

In 1939, Francis married Catherine Bronson, a Gallaudet graduate and a former teacher at the Kentucky School for the Deaf. They have four children and five grandchildren.

Thomas K. Holcomb (A) Tom Holcomb is part of the third generation of Deaf people in his family. He grew up in different parts of the country, including Tennessee, Indiana, and California. One of the results of his family's moving around was that Tom gained a lot of experience with different school systems and communication modes. He went to residential schools, day schools for the deaf, and public schools. In these different schools, he was exposed to oral, manual, and total communication programs.

Tom is a graduate of Gallaudet College. He is currently completing his master's degree requirements in career and human resource development at the College of Applied Science and Technology of Rochester Institute of Technology (RIT). He is also a developmental education specialist at RIT. He works closely with the students on personal/social development and leadership skills development.

Henry Holter (D. 1991) Henry Holter was almost an octogenarian and already a great-grandfather when his story was recorded in the fall of 1982. He has been "watching" Sunday sermons for almost seven decades. He began watching sermons at the North Dakota School for the Deaf. Chapel services were held every school day and on Sunday mornings. Sunday chapel services were also part of the curriculum at Gallaudet College when Henry was a student from 1925 to 1930.

E. Lynn Jacobowitz (A) As the only deaf person in her family, Lynn Jacobowitz, like many other children in similar situations, grew up in an oral environment. She was born and raised in Brooklyn, New York. She attended the Lexington School for the Deaf through the eighth grade. Although Lexington was an oral school, students used sign language in the stairwells, restrooms, and in other areas when teachers and houseparents were not around. Lynn received her high school education (without the assistance of interpreters) at New Utrecht High School.

By the time Lynn matriculated to Gallaudet College, she was competent in sign language. She received her bachelor's degree in psychology in 1976. She obtained a teaching job at the Hilda Knoff School for the Deaf in New Orleans. During her one-and-half years at this school Lynn began writing one- and two-act plays.

In the summer of 1979 Lynn attended a deaf playwrights conference sponsored by the National Theatre of the Deaf. In 1982 she wrote and directed her first full-length play, *Oh, Stop! Oh, Stop!* Through her plays, cartoons, and video-recorded stories, Lynn is able to convey her experiences with oralism versus manualism and Signed English versus American Sign Language. She also reveals some of the intercultural problems between deaf and hearing people.

Lynn is presently a faculty member in the Department of Sign Communication at Gallaudet College. She has conducted numerous workshops on deaf culture, deaf folklore, methods and materials for sign language teachers, and television production. When she is not giving workshops, she is at home in Maryland working on ideas for cartoons and television projects.

Jerald M. Jordan
(H; D. 2008)
Jerald M. Jordan is a 1948 graduate of Gallaudet College. He has been with the college for twenty-one years in various capacities—as an instructor in physics and in mathematics, as founder and first director of the computer center, and currently as director of Admissions and Records.

"JJ," as he is known, has many and varied interests. In addition to his work as a guinea pig for the U.S. Navy, which he describes in his story, he has obtained a private pilot's license, flown solo as far west as Wichita, Kansas, and as far north as Detroit, Michigan. His current interests lie in boating on the Chesapeake Bay. JJ is also president of the International Committee of Sports for the Deaf, which oversees the Deaf Olympics. In this role he and his wife, Shirley, have traveled widely throughout Europe, Japan, and South America.

Barbara Kannapell
(A)
Barbara Kannapell sees herself as a person first, and a deaf person second, through her work as an advocate with Deafpride, Inc. She is the president and co-founder of this community-based organization in Washington, D.C., which advocates human rights among deaf people and their families, and promotes bilingual education for deaf children. Barbara was born into a deaf family—her parents, uncle, and two aunts are all deaf. Her sister is the only hearing member of the family. She is a niece of

the famous George Gordon Kannapell, who was well-known in the deaf community for his humorous antics at NAD rallies in the 1950s. She got many good stories from her deaf relatives.

Barbara travels widely as a lecturer on various topics ranging from advocacy to bilingual education for deaf children. All these topics draw more from her life experiences than from books. She worked as a research assistant at Gallaudet for seventeen years following her graduation from Gallaudet College. She earned a master's degree in educational technology from Catholic University, and she is currently a Ph.D. candidate in sociolinguistics at Georgetown University. She is presently working as a linguistics specialist with the Instructional Development and Evaluation Center at Gallaudet.

Eric Malzkuhn (H; D. 2008) Eric Malzkuhn, better known as "Malz," fell in love with sign language at the age of twelve, and it proved no passing fancy. He is still caressing signs into outlandish

and charming configurations as a drama teacher at the Model Secondary School for the Deaf (MSSD), some 40-odd years later. His first blockbuster was *The Jabberwock*, loosed upon an unsuspecting world when he was seventeen.

Malz taught in Michigan and California. He has also been a printer, advertising copywriter, and vocational rehabilitation field agent. He earned a master's degree in drama from Catholic University. He was the first director to stage a full-fledged musical in sign language—*Oliver*—in 1976 at MSSD. He has worked with interpreters all over the nation and has taught artistic-theatrical sign language in many colleges via workshops and at the National Theatre of the Deaf's summer school program.

Malz's wife, Mary (a Gallaudet political science professor), is studying for her doctorate, and Malz is eagerly anticipating receiving the first letter addressed to "Dr. and Mr. Malzkuhn." Malz and Mary have four boys; one is their dog and one is a deaf son (he's a teacher in California—the son, not the dog). Malz continues his antics on the stage, but his favorite role as an actor was Ben Franklin in *1776*.

Thomas A. Mayes, Ph.D.
(H; D. 1999)
Tom Mayes has lived and worked in many parts of the United States, attended seven different universities, and was mainstreamed in the public schools some 40 years before 94-142 became a law. Presently he is Vice President of the Division of Public Services at Gallaudet College.

Tom became deaf from spinal meningitis at the age of six. He attended the Oregon School for the Deaf for several years before entering the public schools of Baker, Oregon. Except for three years in the fields of journalism and advertising in Chicago, he has spent his entire professional career in the field of education, much of it with the C. S. Mott Foundation in Flint, Michigan. He was on the faculty of California State University at Northridge before coming to Gallaudet. He holds a bachelor's degree from the University of Chicago and a doctorate from Michigan State University.

Carolyn McCaskill
(A)
Carolyn McCaskill grew up in Mobile, Alabama. She is the oldest of five children Her parents are hearing, but two of her sisters and one cousin are deaf.

Carolyn attended Gallaudet College from 1972 to 1977. The highlight of her years at Gallaudet College was being selected as Miss Gallaudet 1976-1978. She was also the first runner-up in the Miss Deaf America pageant. As Miss Gallaudet, she represented Gallaudet College at banquets and club meetings, toured schools for the deaf, and gave speeches and performances to many different groups.

In 1977, Carolyn received her bachelor's degree in psychology and social work from Gallaudet. She received a master's degree in guidance and counseling from Gallaudet in 1979.

Carolyn has worked at the Model Secondary School for the Deaf (MSSD) for five years. She loves working with adolescent students. She feels that she is a positive role model to many of the black deaf students at MSSD. She often tells them that she grew up without seeing any black deaf professionals. Today, these students have many more career opportunities and chances for success than deaf students had in the past. Carolyn urges her students to take advantage of these opportunities.

H. Paul Menkis (D. 2017) Having been "educated by rote" in an oral school (failure), a public school mainstreaming program (failure), public schools (failure), and finally several residential schools (the beginning), Harmon Paul Menkis began his journey into what he considers the "windows of life." Observing that communication was a major key to survival, he noticed that both American Sign Language and English were bridges to communication and survival in each respective culture. He set out towards mastery of both languages in order to have the best of both worlds.

Paul has since been engaged in varied and diverse vocations and avocations ranging from unskilled labor to blue collar, white collar, and professional endeavors. On the ladder to success, he attributes each rung to sheer discipline and to mastery of both American Sign Language and English. He believes the acquisition of skills in imparting these languages to others demands a repertoire of second-language teaching skills, sensitivity, awareness, and acceptance of communication differences among individuals. Paul is considered a master teacher by many of his students. He is currently an assistant professor of Sign Communication in the Gallaudet College School of Communication.

Mary Beth Miller Mary Beth Miller is a well-known figure in theatre productions for the deaf. She became an actress after graduating from Gallaudet College. She is the daughter of deaf parents, and she has a deaf sister.

Mary Beth has been involved in many interesting projects. She co-authored *Handtalk, An ABC Book of Sign Language and Fingerspelling;* she has been involved in the production of *Rainbow's End*, a television series for deaf children and their families; and she is currently active in forming the New York Deaf Theatre in New York City. She will serve as an actress, writer, and director for this group. In addition to her work in theatre and television, Mary Beth has also been active in deaf education. She holds two master's degrees, one in educational theatre and one in deaf education.

Agnes Padden

Agnes Padden is a second-generation Washington, D.C. resident. She has never lived outside of the metropolitan D.C. area. Ms. Padden grew up on Kendall Green. She attended Kendall School, and she became the first Kendall School woman to graduate from Gallaudet College. She has been teaching at Gallaudet since 1947, with some time off to raise a family. She is presently a teacher in the English department at Gallaudet.

Agnes and her husband, Don, enjoy traveling. Their most recent trip was to the Soviet Union. In Washington, Agnes is actively involved in several professional, educational, and social organizations. She also keeps in close contact with her children and their spouses.

Donald Padden

Donald Padden was born to deaf parents in Chicago. He attended the Minnesota School for the Deaf in Faribault. After graduating from Gallaudet College in 1945, he accepted an offer from Dr. Percival Hall (Gallaudet's president) to teach physical education and health at the college. Don is now spending his thirty-ninth year at Gallaudet. He has seen the college change from a small-time college to the well-known institution it is today.

Don likes to travel. He also likes to collect unusual items— conversation pieces. He is a staunch supporter of the Gallaudet College Alumni

Association. He is the editor of the *Mileposts* section in the Gallaudet alumni newsletter, the national treasurer of the GCAA, and the chairman of the Laurent Clerc Cultural Fund Committee.

Don and his wife, Agnes, have two children—Bob, who is coordinator of career education at the Maryland School for the Deaf in Frederick, and Carol, who is teaching at the University of California at San Diego.

Ray S. Parks, Jr.
Considered a "Renaissance" man by many who have known him, Ray S. Parks, Jr., in part, owes his multifaceted experiences and achievements to his admiration for Leonardo da Vinci. He has been recognized for his athletic feats in many sports—he won five consecutive A.A.U. diving championships in Virginia and was a participant in the 1961 and 1965 International Games of the Deaf. He won a bronze medal in high-board diving and a silver medal in wrestling.

Ray is also known for his talents as an actor (he was once with the National Theatre of the Deaf) and an educator. He has presented numerous workshops and lectures in the areas of communication, theatre arts, education of the deaf, and curriculum development; his services continue to be in demand.

A 1960 Gallaudet College graduate, he has begun studies toward his doctorate degree in educational administration at New York University, and he is also an educational director at a school for the deaf.

Frances M. Parsons
(D. 2013)
Frances Margaret (Peggie) Parsons has met people in all walks of life and has traveled around the globe to almost everywhere except New Zealand and the North and South Poles— probably because there are no deaf penguins! Peggie was born prematurely and was not expected to live, but her father nurtured her through the first crucial weeks of her life. She lived in Tahiti during her

teenage years. The experience taught her to value and respect international cultures.

In addition to having private tutors, Peggie attended many different schools, including public schools, the California School for the Deaf, Gallaudet College, Howard University, George Washington University, and the University of Maryland. She earned a master's degree in art history from the University of Maryland. At Gallaudet, she gained insight into the social development, culture, and leadership capabilities of deaf people. This experience had a great impact on her and influenced her on the path toward global ambassadorship for total communication.

Peggie is an assistant professor of art history at Gallaudet. She contributes her vacation time to working with international professionals in education of the deaf. She was instrumental in developing the Peace Corps program for the deaf in the Philippines. She served the Peace Corps as a participant-traveler in the Far East, Kenya, and Seychelles, and as a cross-cultural trainer and recruiter. She has influenced many deaf school pupils and college students from all over the United States in their decisions to become Peace Corps volunteers.

Peggie has received numerous honors and awards from various organizations in Washington, D.C, and in other nations. She has written an autobiography of her life in Tahiti and published countless articles in newspapers and magazines.

Even though she cannot draw, Peggie collects paintings and lithographs from all parts of the world. She has originals by well-known artists on every available wall in her home—enough to compete with art galleries that are only a stone's throw away.

Don G. Pettingill (D. 2005) Don G. Pettingill became deaf at the age of five. He likes to say there was no psychological impact because his father was very hard of hearing and he had eight brothers and sisters who never let him use his deafness as an excuse for anything. They would say: "So you're deaf! So's Dad and he's done pretty well for himself."

As a result, Don grew up with a "so what" attitude about his deafness. At the age of twenty-six, he bought his own commercial printing shop, and he managed it for sixteen years. When the hours became longer and the worries multiplied, he decided to sell. He then served as a rehabilitation specialist for adult deaf people for nine years. During this period, Don started different programs in three large metropolitan areas in as many states.

He graduated from Gallaudet College with a bachelor's degree in psychology in 1976; served as president of the NAD from 1972 to 1974; and developed the original Work Study Program at the Model Secondary School for the Deaf.

At present, Don is director of Programs in Adult and Community Education (PACE) at Gallaudet College.

Nancy Rarus

Nancy Rarus has long been an active member of the deaf community. Her involvement extends to both social and educational realms. The deaf daughter of deaf parents, and the mother of deaf children, Nancy has an intrinsic appreciation of deaf culture. She has spent many years working at improving the quality of life for deaf citizens.

While teaching at the American School for the Deaf, in West Hartford, Connecticut, she was active at both the state and national levels of the NAD; she was coordinator of the In-Service Total Communication Program for the junior high school at the American School; and she established and coordinated the Sign Language Instructor's Pool of Connecticut (SLIP). In addition, Nancy has served on the National Captioning Institute Advisory Board.

Nancy now makes her home in Arizona, where she continues to be active in the deaf community. Her most recent appointment has been as Chairlady of the Community Outreach Program of the Deaf Administrative Advisory Board in Tucson, Arizona.

Roslyn Rosen, Ed.D. Roslyn Rosen was practically born signing to a deaf family in New York City, and she grew up thinking that people who could not sign had a learning problem. Today, she and her brother, Harvey Goodstein, are the only known sister-brother combo to have doctoral degrees. A graduate of Gallaudet College (bachelor's and master's degrees), she continued her education at Catholic University.

Roz is known for her involvement in the deaf community and in the field of deaf education. She currently is the Dean of the College for Continuing Education at Gallaudet College. Positions she has held in the past include teacher, supervising teacher, vocational rehabilitation counselor, coordinator of the Gallaudet P.L. 94-142 effort, and director of the Kellogg-Gallaudet Special School of the Future Project. She has served on several national boards including the NAD and the International Association of Parents of the Deaf.

"Behind every successful woman is a wonderful man and supportive children," says Roz of her husband. Herb, and their children, Jeff, Steve, and Suzy.

Robert G. Sanderson, Ed.D. (H; D. 2012) Robert G. Sanderson— Sandy, as he is known to his friends and colleagues—became deaf at the age of eleven from spinal meningitis during the epidemic of the early thirties. After becoming deaf, he returned to public school, but he couldn't "make it" in the so-called mainstream. He was then sent to the Utah School for the Deaf, from which he graduated. He then went on to Gallaudet College for a B.A., California State University at Northridge for an M.A. in educational administration, then to the University of Utah, and finally to Brigham Young University for a doctoral degree. Along the way he married Mary Antonietti, another graduate of the USD, and they produced two sons.

Sandy left his long-time job as a draftsman to enter the rehabilitation field in 1965.

He became the first full-time coordinator of services to the deaf in the nation. He developed the first rehabilitation unit of services to the deaf, providing a model for other states. Most of the recommendations of the Model State Plan for the Rehabilitation of Deaf Clients were originated and implemented in the Utah program long before other states had coordinators. Sandy also worked as a rehabilitation counselor for the deaf (RCD) and as a supervisor of other RCDs.

Sandy found time to be president of the NAD (1964-1968) and he continued to be active in organizations of and for the deaf in addition to professional organizations. He served as president of the Utah Rehabilitation Administration Association and as a board member of the American Deafness and Rehabilitation Association. At present he is secretary of the Utah Association of the Deaf, a United Way Agency; Western Grand Vice-President and Chairman of the Board of the National Fraternal Society of the Deaf; and director of the new Utah Comprehensive Community Center for the Deaf.

Members of the Gallaudet community will remember Sandy as the 1981-1982 occupant of the Powrie V. Doctor Chair of Deaf Studies. He is currently a member of the Gallaudet Board of Trustees. Among all his achievements, Sandy thinks that his number one is his successful marriage. The total support of his wife, Mary, and sons, Gary and Barry, made it all possible.

Kathleen Schreiber
(D. 1992)
Kathleen Schreiber, better known as Kit, has been the mainstay of the local Washington, D.C, newsletter, DEE CEE EYES, since its conception in 1961 by her late husband, Frederick. He was forever brimming over with new ideas and involving his family, including their four children, in numerous projects.

Kit received her B.A. in English from Gallaudet in 1980. She has published a book of poetry, "Dear Beth, Love, Mom," and is contemplating a second book and a novel in the near future. She has worked for Gallaudet Computer Services for twenty years. She can recall when Gallaudet had a first generation computer, an IBM 1620. She loves to tell stories about the good old days.

Kit lives with her mother in Kensington, Maryland, where they have gained a reputation for growing beautiful roses.

Carl Schroeder (D. 2013)

Carl Schroeder was born in The Hague, The Netherlands. He and his parents moved to the United States when Carl was ten years old. Carl became a U.S. citizen in 1973.

Carl graduated from the Model Secondary School for the Deaf in Washington, D.C. He was the valedictorian of his class. He then attended Gallaudet College. He majored in American Studies. Carl was very active in campus activities. During his sophomore year, he was president of the Student Body Government. During his senior year, he was a visitor's guide at the Gallaudet Visitors Center.

Carl received a Thomas J. Watson Foundation Fellowship at the end of his senior year. The fellowship helps students travel and study in other countries. Carl will spend one year in The Netherlands. He will study the living conditions and activities of deaf people in The Netherlands. He will also visit organizations and rehabilitation centers for deaf adults. Carl is particularly interested in learning about the human rights of the deaf in The Netherlands.

Michael Schwartz, J.D.

Michael Schwartz, deaf since birth, grew up in New Rochelle, New York, where he attended public schools. He received a B.A. in English from Brandeis University, graduating cum laude (with honors). He then obtained a master's degree in theatre from Northwestern University and taught drama at the North Carolina School for the Deaf in Morganton.

Michael has also been a member of the troupe of the National Theatre of the Deaf. After a year of touring the United States with the company, Michael decided that the law offered tremendous tools to aid in the struggle for deaf people's rights, and so he went into hibernation for three years at New York University. He graduated in 1982 from the NYU School of Law with a J.D. degree. He has great hopes for the future and seeks to devote his legal skills to the deaf community.

James M. Searls (A) James M. Searls, known as Matt, is a graduate of Gallaudet College with bachelor and master of arts degrees in social work and counseling, respectively. While he was a student at the Virginia School for the Deaf and the Blind, he participated in dramatics, an activity he continued throughout his college years and into the present.

Matt is a deaf son of hearing parents, brother of deaf and hearing siblings, and husband of a deaf elementary school teacher. During his four years at the Counseling and Placement Center at Gallaudet, he acquired considerable knowledge and skills in career and personal counseling. He is currently the director of the Preparatory

Studies program at Gallaudet. Matt and his wife, Susan, make their home in Cheverly, Maryland.

Cheryl Shevlin Cheryl Shevlin was born in Minnesota. She is the only deaf person in her family. Cheryl went to the Minnesota School for the Deaf in Faribault. Then she attended Gallaudet College, where she received a B.S. in home economics.

Cheryl has taught in several different places. After she graduated from Gallaudet, she obtained a job at the Virginia School for the Deaf in Staunton. From there, she went to Whitney M. Young High School in Chicago, Illinois. After one year in Chicago, Cheryl moved back to Washington, D.C, to become a home economics teacher at Kendall Demonstration Elementary School.

Cheryl has many hobbies and interests outside of teaching. She collects antique dolls and other kinds of antiques. She also has an adventurous spirit. She has visited Sweden, Denmark,

Mexico, and Canada, and she has traveled all over the United States.

Deborah M. Sonnenstrahl (Blumenson) (A) Deborah M. Sonnenstrahl, who now serves as director of the Fine Arts in Education program at Gallaudet College, considers herself to be a "late bloomer." Being a late bloomer, however, has its advantages. One gets to appreciate and cherish the finer points in life much longer.

It was at Gallaudet College that Deborah's life began to blossom. Up to that time she had lived in a relatively tame world, learning to read and speak. When she enrolled at Gallaudet, it was against her own wishes! However, her parents foresaw the advantages of her getting an education on an equal footing with her peers, rather than fighting the hassles in a hearing college. While at Gallaudet College she learned the beauty of sign language, and then there was no stopping her. She grew from a wallflower to a ham on stage, gaining a reputation as an actress, instructor of art history, and an advocate of deaf rights, especially in the area of museums. She later graduated from Catholic University with a master's degree in art history. With her varied interests, she has never lost her sense of beauty.

In her present job, Deborah has done much to further the cause of making museums accessible to deaf people. She has been the recipient of many honors and awards, including the Teacher of the Year award, the Tower Clock award, dedication of the Gallaudet yearbook to her, and "Best Overall Performance by an Actor or Actress" in the Maryland One-Act Play Tournament, in which she competed against hearing actors. She makes her home in the shadow of the Smithsonian Institution complex in Washington, D.C.

Frank R. Turk (A, H) Frank Turk is probably one of the most readily recognizable figures to deaf high school students and young adults in the country today. He has spent his entire professional career actively involved in helping young deaf people become aware of their capabilities and realize their fullest potential.

Frank, a native of Hibbing, Minnesota, became deaf at the age of four from spinal meningitis. He attended the Minnesota School for the Deaf, where he was an active participant in school activities. His participation in school activities, especially sports, continued throughout his college years at Gallaudet College. After graduating from Gallaudet in 1952, Frank became a counselor and the director of extracurricular activities at Kendall School. Between 1965 and 1980 he served as the director of Junior NAD. In this role he traveled across the country, speaking to groups of young deaf people. During these "talks" Frank always stressed the need for deaf youth to develop self-discipline, self-respect, and self-confidence.

Frank is currently the acting director for the Office of Student Life at Gallaudet College, but he still maintains that his first and foremost commitment will always be to the deaf youth of America.

SUGGESTIONS FOR ACTIVITIES

1. VOCABULARY

There are many new vocabulary words found in the stories. The following vocabulary words have been chosen from all thirty-seven stories. Have the students look up the meanings of the word and then have them write sentences using the words appropriately.

acclamation	envy	nominate
allowance	exasperation	nonchalantly
astronaut	exhilarating	nonplussed
barnstorm	exile	paralyzed
bilingual	fantasize	semaphore
chaotic	foreman	sketch
commercial (adj.)	gesundheit	sociolinguistics
crestfallen	letdown	soundtrack
discrimination	liaison	uproar
eaves	mime	weightlessness
eavesdropper	motion sickness	

2. IDIOMS AND EXPRESSIONS

The following idioms and expressions are a sample of those found in the stories. Have the students try to define these phrases from the context of the story. This can be done in a class discussion or individually.

work like a horse	pick someone's brain
pitch hay	mother institution
run of the play	take off like a shot
the Big Top	I can't do that to save my life
perk up	fit into a mold
mustered up his courage	mental crutch
blockhead	a familiy secret
not helping the situation	the tables are turned

3. COMPOSITIONS AND STORIES

The following are suggestions for written compositions or stories that can be told in class.

- Describe a summer job, or an experience at summer camp. Describe a scary situation.
- Describe a dream or fantasy that seemed real.
- Think of some word games to help remember information, i.e., h-o-m-e-s for the Great Lakes.
- Describe a funny incident that happened with a brother/ sister
- Describe a pet, real or imagined.
- Think of some things that hearing people think deaf people can't do, that they really can do.
- Describe the first time you were allowed to go out by yourself.
- Write a story that teaches a lesson or has a moral.
- Write about your goals and aspirations for the future.

4. GROUP PROJECTS

Have the students begin a deaf heritage project to find out the history of deaf people in either their hometowns or the town where the school is located. The project could result in a newsletter or deaf heritage album to add to the school's library collection. (The students may want to refer to "The World Around You," published by Pre-College Programs at Gallaudet College as an example of a student newsletter, and "Deaf Heritage" by Jack R. Gannon as an example of an album.

Have the students interview deaf adults in the community to find out what it was like to grow up deaf, to find out how their school has or hasn't changed, and to find out how community services have changed over the years.

Have the students collect stories and anecdotes from deaf adults. If equipment is available, record the students or adults telling these stories. If equipment is unavailable, have the students or adults present the stories at an assembly program or in a class.

81194495R00119

Made in the USA
Middletown, DE
21 July 2018